FROM THE BIBLE-TEACHING MINISTRY OF
CHARLES R. SWINDOLL

D0596141

INSIGHT'S *Handbook*
OF OLD TESTAMENT
BACKGROUNDS
JOB–MALACHI

KEY CUSTOMS FROM EACH BOOK

INSIGHT'S HANDBOOK OF OLD TESTAMENT BACKGROUNDS
KEY CUSTOMS FROM EACH BOOK, JOB–MALACHI

From the Bible-Teaching Ministry of Charles R. Swindoll

Charles R. Swindoll has devoted his life to the accurate, practical teaching and application of God's Word and His grace. A pastor at heart, Chuck has served as senior pastor to congregations in Massachusetts, California, and Texas. Since 1998, he has served as the founder and senior pastor-teacher of Stonebriar Community Church in Frisco, Texas, but Chuck's listening audience extends far beyond a local church body. As a leading program in Christian broadcasting since 1979, *Insight for Living* airs in major Christian radio markets around the world, reaching people groups in languages they can understand. Chuck's extensive writing ministry has also served the body of Christ worldwide, and his leadership as president and now chancellor of Dallas Theological Seminary has helped prepare and equip a new generation of men and women for ministry. Chuck and Cynthia, his partner in life and ministry, have four grown children, ten grandchildren, and five great-grandchildren.

Published By:
IFL Publishing House
A Division of Insight for Living Ministries
Post Office Box 5000
Frisco, Texas 75034-0055

Editor in Chief: Cynthia Swindoll, President, Insight for Living Ministries
Executive Vice President: Wayne Stiles, Th.M., D.Min., Dallas Theological Seminary
Writers: John Adair, Th.M., Ph.D., Dallas Theological Seminary
Malia Rodriguez, Th.M., Dallas Theological Seminary
Sharifa Stevens, Th.M., Dallas Theological Seminary
Substantive Editor: Kathryn Robertson, M.A., English, Hardin-Simmons University
Copy Editors: Jim Craft, M.A., English, Mississippi College;
Certificate of Biblical and Theological Studies, Dallas Theological Seminary
Paula McCoy, B.A., English, Texas A&M University-Commerce
Project Supervisor, Creative Ministries: Megan Meckstroth, B.S., Advertising, University of Florida
Project Manager, Publishing: Rachael Deatherage, Communications Project Manager,
Insight for Living Ministries
Proofreader: LeeAnna Swartz, B.A., Communications, Moody Bible Institute
Cover Designer: Margaret Gulliford, B.A., Graphic Design, Taylor University
Production Artist: Nancy Gustine, B.F.A., Advertising Art, University of North Texas
Photos: Wayne Stiles: page 12
Todd Bolen/BiblePlaces.com: page 54
WikiMedia Commons Images:
Giovanni Dall'Orto: page 64

ISBN: 978-1-62655-103-9
Printed in the United States of America

TABLE OF CONTENTS

APPENDIX

A NOTE FROM CHUCK SWINDOLL

Have you ever watched a five-year-old try to figure out how to use a rotary phone? Or given some Wite-Out to a teenager to fix a mistake on a term paper? Chances are, those kids had no idea what you'd just handed them . . . no idea how to use these everyday items that we adults grew up with. Corded phones with rotary dialers have been relegated to the dusty annals of history, along with typewriters and tools made to correct typed or handwritten errors. Our phones have gotten smarter. Our ability to document our thoughts now comes with backspace buttons and auto-correct. We are *way* past the Wite-Out days.

Yet some things never change. We still long to connect, whether it's through a phone call, text, tweet, status update, or video chat. We make mistakes that need fixing. And there will always, *always* be homework.

Context matters. Without context, it's difficult to interpret the function and meaning behind an object or a custom—to understand what's changed and what hasn't. Context is never more critical than when reading the Bible. It's easy to dismiss the unfamiliar with a shrug and a "Who knows?" But to avoid the worthy work of contextualization is to dismiss the Scriptures. When we do that, we miss God-breathed truths that apply to *all* God's people throughout time.

The resource you hold in your hand—*Insight's Handbook of Old Testament Backgrounds: Key Customs from Each Book, Job–Malachi*—will give you the cultural grounding you need to read the Bible the way God intended. Have you ever wondered about the function of casting lots? What life was like for hired servants? What "cast your bread upon the waters" means? This handbook will provide clear, concise explanations for all of these and many more unfamiliar, Old Testament concepts. You'll find yourself thumbing through it again and again.

May God deepen your pursuit of a broader understanding of His Word, and may you find great value in this helpful study aid.

Chuck Swindoll

Charles R. Swindoll

HOW TO USE THIS BOOK

Plan to use this volume alongside your copy of Scripture.

We have organized the topics by the verse and Bible book in which they appear. Many Bible books cover the same topics, so in an effort to avoid repetition, we've included both a **Scripture index** and a **subject index**. So when some detail from, say, Psalms strikes you, search our indexes in the back of the book to see where we've dealt with the topic.

We hope you'll find this a helpful way to explore the wide array of interesting Bible backgrounds and cultural insights presented in this book.

INSIGHT'S *Handbook*
OF OLD TESTAMENT
BACKGROUNDS

JOB–MALACHI

JOB

1:2−3   How Wealth was Measured

Of all the men in Uz, which was most likely located outside Canaan, Job was the wealthiest. In his day, wealth consisted most often of abundant crops, livestock, and other forms of food. In fact, food was the most important "currency" in ancient Israel. Survival in the ancient Near East depended on a good harvest, which required land to grow the crops and animals to plow the fields and bring in the harvest. Job had all the resources necessary to produce abundant food for his family and also to sell to others. He had five hundred pairs of oxen that plowed his fields and gave milk. In addition, his thousands of sheep provided food and wool for clothing, while his plentiful camels and donkeys provided transportation.[1]

Abraham, who lived in roughly the same time period as Job, was a wealthy businessman. He had silver, gold, flocks, herds, and servants in abundance. The land required for Abraham's livestock was so great that he had to separate from his nephew, Lot, who also had many animals and servants (Genesis 13:2−6). In the ancient Near East, the rich also had luxurious clothing, like the beautiful garments Joseph sent back from Egypt to his father (45:22). By Solomon's day, the wealthy also had abundant horses, chariots, and access to expensive imported items such as ivory (2 Chronicles 9:17, 25).

1:3   Job's Servants

Job not only owned thousands of animals and the land necessary to keep them; he also had many servants. The Hebrew word translated "servant" sometimes indicates a person who was regarded as property but more often refers to one who had pledged allegiance to his or her master.

Job 1:3 uses a term that is best translated as "servant." [2] The system of servanthood in ancient Israel was likely much different than what comes to the minds of modern-day readers when they think about slavery. To understand this more fully, consider that Genesis 26:14 uses the same Hebrew word as Job 1:3 when describing Isaac's wealth but translates it as "great household." The implication? Masters like Job and Isaac considered their servants part of the family. And these men's character, wisdom, and godly fear indicate that they likely treated their servants with respect and justice rather than as possessions.

Later, with the advent of the Mosaic Law, God prohibited His people from buying other Hebrews to be slaves (Leviticus 25:42). But those who did become servants were to receive certain protections and considerations: they were to be released after six years of service (Exodus 21:1–11); they were to receive wages; and they could not be treated with severity (Leviticus 25:39–55).

3:8; 40:15; 41:1   Sea Monsters and Land Beasts

While *Leviathan* in Job 3:8 may refer to a powerful, fear-inspiring crocodile as it does in Job 41, it most likely points to Lotan, the seven-headed dragon of Canaanite mythology. According to the myth, when Lotan arose in the daytime, it swallowed the sun and caused an eclipse. If the sun had failed to shine on Job's birthday, the day, in a sense, would never have existed. Lotan represented evil, chaos, and darkness in the ancient Near East. [3] Job's reference to this Canaanite myth doesn't indicate that he believed in Lotan but rather that he felt as if his life had been engulfed with grief and pain. Job's misery was so bad he employed a hyperbole that the mythological Lotan had swallowed up all light and life and hope and left him in darkness.

The powerful Nile crocodile, revered in Job's day, was no match for God.

In Job 41:1, Job used the mythological name "Leviathan" to refer to the Nile crocodile. Job's detailed description of the Nile crocodile's frame, skin, scales, teeth, eyes, and mouth shows that Job spoke about an actual animal as opposed to the mythical creature in Job 3:8. The Nile crocodile lived in the Nile River, although some remains have been found near Mount Carmel and the Zerka River near Caesarea. The crocodile in Job's day was larger than modern-day crocodiles. These creatures were revered in Egypt and even raised and kept in pagan temples. And because crocodiles often fed on dead animals, the Israelites regarded them as unclean. [4]

In Job 40:15, God asked Job if he could control another peculiar creature: the powerful behemoth. The Hebrew word *behemoth* means "beast" and probably referred to the hippopotamus, which lived in the Nile River. Scripture's detailed description of the creature's diet, physical attributes, and habitat points to a literal beast rather than a mythical one. [5]

Related passages: Psalm 74:14; 104:26; Isaiah 27:1

Ancient caravans provided safety in numbers when traversing dangerous landscapes.

6:19   Ancient Transportation

In the ancient Near East, those who traveled to conduct trade or for other purposes often went in caravans or large groups of people and pack animals. Travel routes in Job's time often traversed dangerous terrain and hostile regions, and caravans provided safety in numbers.[6] Because Job owned many pack animals and servants and likely conducted trade, he was familiar with journeying in caravans. When he compared his so-called friends to the caravans who traveled from Tema in northern Arabia to Sheba in southwestern Arabia—whose search for water proved futile[7]—he highlighted their failure as friends. Rather than providing safety or helping him journey to the refreshing "waters" he so desperately needed, Job's "friends" brought him only dangerous and disappointing advice.

Ancient caravans often had a leader who determined the road they would follow and made business decisions to buy and sell along the way. When a caravan of Ishmaelite traders on their way to Egypt passed Joseph's brothers as they tended their father's sheep, the brothers sold Joseph to the Ishmaelites (Genesis 37:28).

Many ancient transportation routes followed the paths of dried up rivers or the trails formed by shepherds moving sheep and cattle. But as trade across Canaan increased, the need for roads increased. Canaan sat at the crossroads of three continents. Caravans traveling between Mesopotamia and Egypt had to travel through Canaan, and caravans from nations to the east had to pass through Canaan to get to the port cities on the Mediterranean. The King's Highway and the Via Maris, two of the primary north-south roads in biblical times, connected Damascus in the north to Egypt and Saudi Arabia in the south. Several other roads connected regions in the east and the west. [8]

Related passages: Genesis 24:10; Numbers 20:17

7:6   How Quick Is a Weaver's Shuttle?

After Job lost everything and faced the pain of an incurable skin disease, he realized the short duration of his life, which was "swifter than a weaver's shuttle" (Job 7:6). The art of weaving involves stretching vertical threads (the warp) on a loom and weaving horizontal threads (the woof or weft) over and under the vertical threads. The "shuttle" Job referenced is a small piece of wood that carries the woof or weft back and forth across the warp. Skilled weavers threw the shuttle back and forth very quickly. Today, to say something is "warp and woof" means that thing is foundational to a system. Weaving itself constituted part of the "warp and woof" of Job's ancient Near Eastern culture.

The earliest paintings of very advanced weaving looms date back to 2000 BC in Egypt, but the craft of weaving dates back even farther. Ancient weavers used wool, silk, and goats' hair. Hebrew weavers most likely learned the art in Egypt and passed the craft down to later generations. [9]

Related passages: Exodus 36:35–38; 1 Samuel 17:7

The papyrus plant provided the raw materials for ancient paper.

8:11   Papyrus Paper

Today, papyrus grows primarily in Sudan and in the marshes in Galilee. In Job's day, the plant grew in marshes of the Nile River in Egypt and was used to make paper. In fact, the word *paper* comes from the word *papyrus*. After the hard outer covering of the stem was removed, paper-makers pressed the inner fibers of the papyrus plant together in vertical strips. They then laid horizontal strips of papyrus fiber on top of the vertical strips, held them together with a glue-like adhesive, and left them to dry in the sun. Placing horizontal fibers on top of the vertical fibers reinforced the resulting "paper" and made it stronger.

Before writing on the papyrus paper, writers rubbed it to make it smooth. The Egyptians started making and writing on papyrus paper at least as early as about 2800–2250 BC. Most papyrus rolls were about thirty feet in length (probably the length of the book of Isaiah), although some Egyptian literary works filled papyrus rolls up to 133 feet long. The Jews, who used the standard thirty-foot rolls, had to divide the Torah into five rolls or "books." [10]

Related passage: Isaiah 18:2

28:16–19   Precious Things

Precious stones, metals, minerals, and materials, like the ones Job mentioned, were as hard to find and as valuable as wisdom and held significant meaning in the ancient Near Eastern world. Job listed seven such elements that often looked much different than they do today:

Coral: The Hebrew word for *coral* means "high" and refers to something with a high value. Used a number of times in the Old Testament, the word could have referred to rubies, pink pearls, garnets, or red coral found in the Mediterranean and Red Seas. The Egyptians used polished red coral in jewelry.[11]

Crystal: The Hebrew word for *crystal* actually means "ice" and refers to hard, transparent, colorless materials. When Scripture refers to crystal, it denotes a brilliant, clear substance, not crystal as modern-day scientists would classify it.[11]

Glass: The Egyptians and Phoenicians discovered how to make glass as early as the third millennium BC. Early glass wasn't clear like most glass today but opaque. Egyptians and Phoenicians used glass to make bracelets, beads, and decorative bottles.[12]

Gold: The gold that Job talked about in Job 28:17 was not refined gold but gold ore that takes hard work to dig out of the earth. Gold ore had some uses in the ancient Near East but, like today, it had the most value after it was refined and purified.[11]

Onyx: The Hebrew word for *onyx* indicates a stone with bands of transparent white with black or other very dark colors. Onyx stones adorned the priests' ephods and breastplates.[11]

Sapphire: Sapphires in Job's day were not like sapphires today but were opaque stones that varied in color from light to dark blue. Such stones are known today as lapis lazuli. When the Old Testament speaks of sapphires, it most likely indicates an assortment of blue stones. Egyptians and Babylonians used lapis lazuli "sapphires" in jewelry.[11]

Topaz: When the Old Testament mentions topaz, it actually refers to modern-day chrysolite, a yellowish-green gem.[11]

Related passages: Exodus 28:6–20; Revelation 21:15–21

30:10; 32:6   Spitting Mad

In the midst of his suffering, the once-respected Job saw the reproachful stares of his friends and heard the snickers of those younger than him (Job 30:1). Although Job lived in a culture where the young venerated their elders and deferred to them in everything, even the young Elihu spoke up to condemn Job (32:6–10).

In addition to being verbally humiliated before those who had once sought his wisdom, Job endured the ultimate dishonor—the cold saliva of cruel people running down his face. In Job's society, spitting in some-one's face was the ultimate sign of disrespect and dishonor. At the gate where he once sat judging with wisdom the cases of his fellow citizens, Job later sat alone as young and old alike approached him only to spit in his face (29:7; 30:10). Earlier in the text, Job reflected on his days as an elder, when young men stood in reverence and dared not look him in the eyes (29:8). Being openly rebuked without restraint by youths may have stung Job even more than the oozing boils that covered his body.

41:7   How to Catch a Fish

To stifle Job's emerging self-righteousness, God reminded him that only the Creator has the power and knowledge to govern all creation. He alone can fish for and catch Leviathan, the great crocodile.

Because of the many lakes and rivers containing many varieties of fish, fishing was and is a common trade in Israel and the ancient Near East. Job chapter 41 mentions two fishing methods: *angling*, which uses a hook and bait to ensnare a fish (Job 41:1), and *spearing*, which uses a spear or harpoon to catch fish (41:7).

Fixed gill nets are nets for catching fish in shallow intertidal zones.

The Bible also mentions one other fishing method, *netting*. In netting, fishermen either throw a mesh net into the water and then draw up the edges of the net, thus trapping fish inside, or they spread the net, which usually measures fifteen feet in diameter, between two boats, and then drop the net into the water. The two boats then drag the net to shore, trapping fish inside.[13]

In Nehemiah 13:16, businessmen from Tyre on the Mediterranean coast caught, transported, and sold fish to the inhabitants of Jerusalem. While many people in biblical times fished to provide food for their families, fishing was also a business.

Related passages: Matthew 4:18–21; Luke 5:1–6; John 21:6–8

42:15 Unique Daughters

While the Bible doesn't tell the names of Job's seven new sons, it does record his three new daughters' names, as well as the fact that Job gave his daughters an inheritance along with their brothers.

Mosaic Law required fathers to give an inheritance to their sons as a means of passing down the family name (Numbers 27:3–4). Mosaic Law only permitted a daughter to receive an inheritance if her father had no sons; this would thus carry on the family name (27:5–8). The inheritance was meant to be kept within one's tribe. If a father had no sons and his daughter received the inheritance and then married outside the tribe, the family inheritance and possibly the family name would be absorbed by another tribe. So the Mosaic Law prohibited daughters who had received an inheritance from marrying outside their tribe (36:3).

Daughters with brothers didn't go without provision. They received a substantial dowry from their fathers when they married.[14] The fact that Job was a blameless and upright man who would not have violated God's Law shows that Job most likely lived during the time of the patriarchs, before the Mosaic Law. Job's actions also illustrate his generosity and grace toward his daughters.

Related passages: Exodus 22:16; 1 Kings 9:16

PSALMS

———❈———

Prayers for Every Season

The book of Psalms models God-honoring prayers for every situation and season of life.

In the *praise psalms*, the psalmist focused on God's role as creator and His mighty works in Israel's history. Some of these were written for temple worship while others reflect personal praise. Psalm 136, for temple worship, recalls God's role as creator and Israel's deliverer and calls worshipers to praise Him.[1]

The *lament psalms*, which express both sorrow and praise, follow a pattern: an address to God; the reason for lament; a confession of trust in God; a petition for God's intervention; and a concluding vow to praise God after He answers. There are two kinds of lament psalms: community (Psalm 60) and individual (Psalm 38).[2]

Thanksgiving psalms have two essential components: an explanation of a crisis and a declaration of deliverance by God. These psalms can be divided into psalms of communal (Psalm 65) and individual (Psalm 118) thanksgiving.[3]

Psalms of trust declare trust in the midst of crisis, but unlike thanksgiving psalms, these psalms do not describe the crisis. In Psalm 23, David proclaims his faith in the midst of his enemies without describing the specific situation.[4]

The *royal psalms* all refer to the "king" or the "anointed one" and to David. These psalms include 2, 18, 20, 21, 45, 72, 89, 101, 110, 132, and 144. Some of these have messianic overtones in that they speak of King David but also look forward to the Messiah.[5]

Some suggest the Israelites would sing the Psalms of Ascent as they climbed the Southern Steps on their pilgrimages to Jerusalem.

The *psalms of the heavenly king* proclaim God's kingship and contain concern for all people; mentions of other gods; God's acts as judge and ruler; and the appropriate physical and spiritual posture of praise before God. These psalms include 47, 93, and 95–99.[6]

The *wisdom psalms* contain divine approval for certain actions (Psalm 1:1); an address to readers as children (34:11); proverbial wisdom (37:1); similes (37:2); truths based on nature (37:9); or comparisons of two things with different levels of value (37:16).[7]

The *Torah psalms* celebrate the value of meditating on and living by God's Law. These psalms reflect on God's ways, works, and words. Only Psalms 1, 19, and 119 can be considered Torah psalms because they are the only ones that focus solely on the Torah. However, many others mention the value of God's Law.[8]

The Israelites would sing the *Psalms of Ascent* (Psalms 120–134) during their pilgrimages to Jerusalem for the three annual feasts — Passover, Pentecost, and Tabernacles (Deuteronomy 16:16). These psalms commemorate God's faithfulness, forgiveness, and provision.

The *imprecatory psalms* use harsh language, calling for God to judge enemies. Imprecatory psalms include 35, 55, 59, 79, 109, and 137. These psalms reveal the psalmists' raw emotions and their trust in God's justice.[9]

A Glossary of Musical Terms[10]

- *Higgaion*: the instruction to include a stringed instrument; seen in Psalm 92:3

- *Lamenasseah*: a directive meaning, "to excel, endure, shine," which could mean to glorify and extol God; applied to fifty-five psalms

- *Maskil*: literally, "making wise or skillful"; scholars differ on what the term means in context but note that the psalms that include the word (32, 42, 44–45, 52–55, 74, 78, 88–89, and 142) may refer either to a specific literary style or to the writer's expression of humility and discipline.

- *Miktam*: probably an Akkadian loanword meaning "to cover"; the psalms associated with miktams (16, 56–60) address the need for atonement and a desire to be defended by God.

- *Mizmor*: the basic term for a melody or poem that is sung with musical accompaniment

- *Selah*: an obscure word that occurs seventy-five times in the psalms; scholars posit that selah is a place-marker.

- *Shiggaion*: a mysterious term used in Psalm 7:1 as well as Habakkuk 3:1, which can speak to the passion of the poem it precedes or define the psalm as a lament

- *Sir*: a "song"

- *Tellehim*: the collection of psalms

Related passages: Psalm 3:1–2; 9:16; 16:1; 32:1

Date palm branches with ripe dates

1:3 Have Some Fruit

The psalmist likened the righteous to well-watered, fruitful trees. In ancient Israel, grapevines, olive trees, and fig trees were some of the most important fruit-bearing plants, and the Bible mentions these many times between Genesis and Revelation. Fruit-bearing plants produce best when their root systems grow deep and have adequate water and nourishment. It's no wonder, therefore, that the Bible often refers to Israel as vines (Psalm 80:8), olives (Jeremiah 11:16), and figs (Luke 13:6–9), indicating the people's need to sink their spiritual roots deep into the soil of God's Word and be continually nourished by His Spirit. Otherwise, like plants without strong roots and water, they would become barren and wither.

Other native fruits found in ancient Israel included: apples, apricots, blackberries, watermelons, mulberries, dates, pomegranates, oranges, lemons, and locust beans. Although almonds are technically seeds, almond trees, which are the first to bloom in Israel, also contributed to springtime produce (Jeremiah 1:11–12).[11]

12:6   Metal Testers

In the ancient Near East, metallurgists worked to refine and purify metals. Metallurgy began before 4000 BC with the hammering and shaping of iron and copper. Between 4000 and 3000 BC, metallurgists hammered and shaped silver and melted and casted copper alloys. By 3000–2000 BC, they started smelting together metals like copper and tin and making gold leaf and metal wire. By 1200 BC, they could make steel. After 1000 BC, metallurgists began welding iron and steel into weapons and tools, as well as stamping bronze coins.

Psalm 12:6 refers to refining silver in the furnace, a process that may have been used first by the Babylonians. After metallurgists smelted silver ores with iron in a hot furnace, they used a blast of air and the heat of the furnace to bring iron and other metal impurities to the surface. These impurities were then either skimmed off or absorbed by the bone ash on which the silver-iron alloy sat. Only pure silver remained.[12]

Related passage: Jeremiah 6:27

23:1   Shepherding 101

The first of the Bible's many shepherds was Abel (Genesis 4:2). Both men and women in Israel worked as shepherds, including David before he became king. But shepherding was a humble profession. In fact, the Egyptians despised shepherds and considered them unclean. When Joseph's shepherd brothers came to eat with him, they were not allowed to sit with the Egyptians (46:34).

Each day, shepherds took their flocks to pasture by walking before them and calling to them. The sheep recognized and followed the shepherd's voice until they reached pastures for food and streams for water. In addition to providing food, shepherds sought out wandering sheep (Ezekiel 34:2) and rescued their flock from predators (Amos 3:12). At the end of each day, the shepherd led his sheep back home, holding his

Shepherds cared for and protected their sheep.

rod over the entrance to the fold so he could account for each sheep (Leviticus 27:32). At night, he guarded them by sitting by the door of the pen (John 10:7).

Shepherds were sometimes divided into regular shepherds and chief shepherds who had charge over others (Genesis 47:6). All shepherds faced danger from predators and endured extreme temperatures (31:40). They wore leather coats lined with fleece in cold weather and carried slingshots and staffs with crooks at the end, which they also used to keep wandering sheep close.[13]

Related passages: Jeremiah 31:10; John 10:33

23:5   Greasy Guys

Many peoples in the ancient Near East, including Egyptians, Hebrews, Greeks, and Romans, used oil on the body much like we use lotion—to keep the skin hydrated in a hot climate. People also used oil to cleanse themselves when they bathed and washed (Ruth 3:3). The use of oil indicated joy (Psalm 23:5), whereas refraining from it often indicated mourning or sadness (Daniel 10:3). Oil was also used to treat some illnesses (Isaiah 1:6; James 5:14) and to anoint the bodies of the dead (Mark 14:8).

Oil had more than practical purposes, however. Jacob used oil to consecrate the stone at Bethel to memorialize his vision of the heavenly stairway. Exodus 30:23–33 gave instructions to priests for anointing certain items for sacred purposes. Oil was also used to anoint the kings of Israel (1 Samuel 10:1; 16:13).[14]

45:8   You Smell Great!

Cosmetics counters, pharmacies, and even our personal vanities are filled with varieties of fragrances to suit our moods and please our senses. But the psalmists didn't just share an obsession with an ancient Near Eastern version of Chanel No. 5. In the Old Testament era, fragrances served as olfactory markers of vitality and attraction as they do today. Women sourced perfume from frankincense, myrrh, nard, cinnamon, and lesser known stacte and galbanum. Perfume extraction was so precious that fragrance itself was traded like currency and a sign of wealth (Genesis 37:25)[15]—the stuff of kings, just as Psalm 45:8 described. But fragrances also served sacred functions. For example, in Exodus 30, God created a recipe for holy anointing oil and incense that could be made only by a professional perfumer—a signature fragrance to signify the set-apart nature of the temple. God forbade the holy recipe from everyday use.

The New Testament also refers to fragrance in connection with the sacred. Mary anointed Jesus with expensive nard (John 12:3), and Paul metaphorically called the knowledge of Jesus a "sweet aroma" and Christian witnesses "the fragrance of Christ" (2 Corinthians 2:14–16).

Related passages: Exodus 30:22–38; Song of Solomon 1:3; 4:10

49:14–15   Sheol

Ancient Israel lacked a fully-developed theology of life after death. However, the Old Testament does include hints of life—including a living physical body—beyond this world in the examples of Enoch (Genesis 5:24) and Elijah (2 Kings 2:11). In addition, 1 Samuel 28:11–19 depicts an intriguing account of Saul talking to Samuel *after* Samuel's death, through conjuring by the medium of En-dor—a practice forbidden by Mosaic Law (Deuteronomy 18:10–11).

The ancient Israelites believed in the afterlife, which they called Sheol—the destination of the dead in the Old Testament. Sheol was the place the dead went "to [their] fathers" (Genesis 15:15) and experienced relief from sickness and pain like David's son did in 2 Samuel 12:23. [16] Notably, Sheol was not equated exclusively with eternal punishment; both the righteous and the unrighteous went to Sheol, though to different areas (see chart on page 19). In Psalm 49:14–15, the psalmist hoped that the corrupt rich would go to Sheol quickly so that the righteous would be delivered from their evil. The psalmist contrasted the short-term prosperity and hubris of the rich with God's ever-faithful protection of the righteous. Though Sheol was the universal destination of the dead, the vindication of the righteous before and after death was a common theme in the psalms.

The New Testament translates *Sheol* as "Hades" (Matthew 11:23; Luke 10:15; Revelation 20:13–14). Originally, *Hades* was the Greek term for "the place of the dead," but its definition expanded in the New Testament to become synonymous with the temporary abode of unbelievers before they are cast forever into the lake of fire (Revelation 20:14).

Related passages: Genesis 37:35; Numbers 16:33; Deuteronomy 32:22; Job 7:9; Psalm 9:17; 16:10; 139:8; Proverbs 5:5; 15:11; Song of Solomon 8:6; Isaiah 14:9; 38:10; Hosea 13:14; Amos 9:2; Habakkuk 2:5

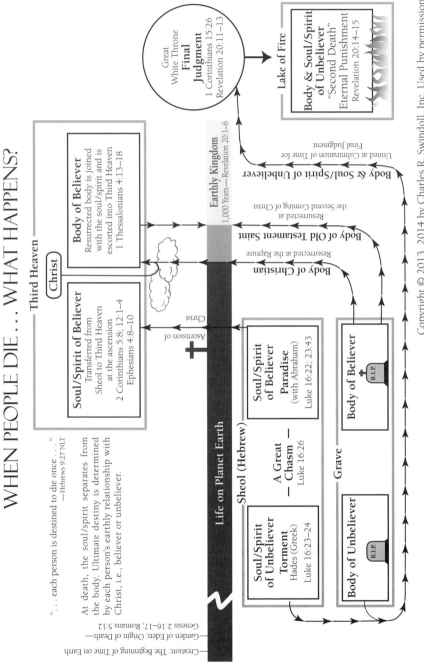

WHEN PEOPLE DIE . . . WHAT HAPPENS?

"... each person is destined to die once ..."
—Hebrews 9:27 NLT

At death, the soul/spirit separates from the body. Ultimate destiny is determined by each person's earthly relationship with Christ, i.e., believer or unbeliever.

—Garden of Eden: Origin of Death—
Genesis 2:16–17; Romans 5:12

Creation: The Beginning of Time on Earth

Third Heaven

Christ

Body of Believer
Resurrected body is joined with the soul/spirit and is escorted into Third Heaven
1 Thessalonians 4:13–18

Soul/Spirit of Believer
Transferred from Sheol to Third Heaven at the ascension
2 Corinthians 5:8; 12:1–4
Ephesians 4:8–10

Ascension of Christ

Soul/Spirit of Believer
Paradise
(with Abraham)
Luke 16:22; 23:43

Body of Believer
R.I.P.

Soul/Spirit of Unbeliever
Torment
Hades (Greek)
Luke 16:23–24

Body of Unbeliever
R.I.P.

— A Great Chasm —
Luke 16:26

Sheol (Hebrew)

Life on Planet Earth

Grave

Great White Throne **Final Judgment**
1 Corinthians 15:26
Revelation 20:11–13

Lake of Fire

Body & Soul/Spirit of Unbeliever
"Second Death" Eternal Punishment
Revelation 20:14–15

Earthly Kingdom
1,000 Years — Revelation 20:1–6

United at Culmination of Time for Final Judgment
Body & Soul/Spirit of Unbeliever

Resurrected at the Second Coming of Christ
Body of Old Testament Saint

Resurrected at the Rapture
Body of Christian

Hyssop

51:7 Hyssop Shower Gel?

Hyssop enjoyed a ubiquitous presence in Israel. These delicately, sweetly scented, bushy plants grew vigorously throughout Israel and played a pivotal part in the nation's cleansing rituals.[17] However, when the Bible speaks of "cleansing" among God's people, it has little to do with the showers, baths, and other means we use to clean ourselves today.

Hyssop makes its first biblical appearance in Exodus 12:22 as the paint brush the Israelites used to mark their doors with the blood of a slain lamb—the first Passover conducted as part of the escape from Egypt. Later, Mosaic Law called for hyssop to be tied with a scarlet string to cedar wood and an animal sacrifice; the bundled items were then used to cleanse people, homes, and the household of God (Leviticus 14:4, 6, 49, 51, 52). In this ritual, hyssop helped sprinkle and distribute the sacrificed animal's blood, mixed with water, and thereby translated a

Jerusalem as Zion, the "city of David" (1 Kings 8:1). Originally, "Zion" probably referred to the walled city that sat on one of the hills in southeast Jerusalem. The ark of the covenant first dwelled in the tent which David set up in Zion (2 Samuel 6:17); therefore, the name developed spiritual significance. While God's people lived in Babylon as captives, Jeremiah encouraged them by repeating God's promise to bring them back home—to Zion (Jeremiah 31:6).

Spiritually, Zion signified God's power and provision of salvation (Psalm 87:5–6), as well as His family relationship with those who are His children through faith (Isaiah 4:2–6). This relationship pointed forward to Christ's provision of salvation through His death and resurrection.[21] When Christ returns, He will do so in Jerusalem (Zechariah 14:1–5) and make His abode on Mount Zion (Revelation 14:1).

84:1   Who Were the Sons of Korah?

Psalms 42, 45–49, 84–85, and 87–88 are attributed to the sons of Korah, the descendants of Levi's son Kohath. Two generations before Korah, God appointed the sons of Kohath to take care of "the ark, the table, the lampstand, the altars, and the utensils of the sanctuary with which they minister, and the screen, and all the service concerning them" (Numbers 3:31). Kohath's grandson, Korah, motivated by pride, led a rebellion against Moses and Aaron because he and some other family members wanted to serve as priests along with Aaron (16:1–35).

Later, Korah's sons became musicians who arranged psalms and sang them as part of Israel's public worship (2 Chronicles 20:19). The sons of Korah, also known as Korahites, were gatekeepers in the temple (1 Chronicles 26:1, 19), just as their forefathers had been keepers of the entrance to the tabernacle in the wilderness (9:19).

91:5–6   Disease and War

Although diseases like Ebola, SARS, and influenza sometimes wreak havoc in the modern world, most in Western society enjoy immunity from or specialized treatment for diseases that once destroyed entire populations. We take for granted routine hygienic practices like hand-washing, sterilizing surgical instruments, laundering sheets, cleansing eating utensils, and isolating those who are infectious. However, up to World War I, none of these habits were commonplace.

Historically, war provided a particularly poor hygienic environment. In the ancient Near East, chronic diarrhea, staph infections, and gangrene plagued soldiers because of a lack of soap, limited access to water, water contamination, and close proximity to dead bodies and infected comrades. The "pestilence that stalks in darkness" (Psalm 91:6) and the "arrow that flies by day" (91:5) were partners in the decimation of people—on both sides of the battle. The Lord's commands regarding cleanliness, such as His instructions for the disposal of human waste in Deuteronomy 23:12–14, were literally lifesaving.

Siege warfare, which involved entrapping populations within their city walls, hastened the grim reality of death through an unhygienic environment. Decaying bodies, hastily buried or unburied, attracted rats and fleas, which fed on corpses and spread infection. Deuteronomy 32 speaks of God's wrath being poured out against His idolatrous people through deaths caused by battle, vermin, and plagues during siege warfare with a "foolish nation" (Deuteronomy 32:21–25).

Related passage: Leviticus 26:14–25

92:12   The Wood Standard

Mentioned often in the Old Testament, palm trees were of great value in the ancient Near East because their sloping height and generously wide leaves provided ample shade from the sun's heat. The foot of a palm tree, therefore, was a natural and popular place to rest and gather (Judges 4:5). Jericho earned the nickname "city of palm trees" (Deuteronomy 34:3; 2 Chronicles 28:15) because the desirable trees could be found in abundance there. When the psalmist compared the righteous person to a palm in Psalm 92:12–14, he likely had in mind palm trees' natural ruggedness and ability to withstand heavy winds and extreme heat.

In the Old Testament, cedars of Lebanon—as building materials—represented majesty and opulence. These trees, called *erez* in Hebrew, pierced and swept the sky with branches that could grow to more than 110 feet across and trunk circumferences that could extend 40 feet.[22] Generation after generation could watch the same cedar grow to maturity over hundreds of years. The psalmist compared the righteous person to this sturdy tree due to its reputation of toughness and endurance—symbols of stability and steadfastness.

Related passages: Judges 9:15; 1 Kings 6:29, 32, 35; 7:36; 2 Chronicles 3:5; Psalm 29:5; 72:16; 104:16; Song of Solomon 7:7–8; Isaiah 2:13; 14:8; Ezekiel 31:3; 41:18–20, 25–26; Hosea 14:5–6

Cedars of Lebanon can withstand both heat and wind.

104:18   Shepha-who?

The word *shephanim* may conjure images of giants—like the *Nephilim*—or the "burning" angelic beings who serve at Yahweh's throne—the *seraphim*. In reality, however, shephanim are neither gigantic nor angelic. They are tiny, furry animals with hardy dispositions that dwell in parts of Africa and the Middle East. They bear resemblance to well-muscled, large guinea pigs crossbred with mice, with miniature versions of rhinoceros molars and hooved, clawed suction cups for feet. What squirrels are to Western parks and wooded areas, shephanim, also translated as "dassies," "conies," or "hyraxes," are to the clefts of the rocks in their homelands.[23] These little creatures have an amazing capability to traverse the most gravity-defying crannies. The psalmist referenced these animals, well-known to his audience, in his illustration of God's provision for and oversight of nature. Just as the storks, the mountain goats, the moon, and the sun have their appointed places, so, too, the tiny, tough shephanim have homes appointed by God (Psalm 104:17–19).

Related passage: Proverbs 30:26

118:22   The Cornerstone

In ancient architecture, the cornerstone was a builder's starting point. "The cornerstone . . . was the largest and or most important stone in the foundation. All the other foundation stones were laid and aligned in reference to this key stone."[24] The larger and more ornate the structure, the more sizeable the cornerstone, because this special stone's purpose was to stand as foundational support for the adjoining walls. In Near Eastern culture, the cornerstone was sacred. Canaanites held human sacrifices and buried the remains underneath the cornerstone in order to consecrate it.[25]

Today, cornerstones have become ceremonious, often featuring inscriptions and time capsules. However, the concept of a cornerstone as the rock upon which an entity stands remains the same, making "the cornerstone" a ubiquitous English expression to indicate someone or something's essential quality. Jesus drew upon that symbolism when He likened Himself to the chief cornerstone (Matthew 21:42; Mark 12:10; Luke 20:17). In Ephesians 2:20, Paul alluded to Psalm 118 to emphasize that Jesus is the pivotal and essential starting point and strength of the Christian faith.

Related passages: Job 38:6; Isaiah 28:16; Zechariah 10:4; Acts 4:11; 1 Peter 2:7

119   The ABCs of Acrostics

Psalm 119 is the longest love letter in the Bible . . . written to commemorate the psalmist's love for God's Word. Psalm 119's 176 verses school readers in the subject of the Word by a clever use of letters known as an acrostic. Webster defines *acrostic* as "a composition usually in verse in which sets of letters (as the initial or final letters of the lines) taken in order form a word or phrase or a regular sequence of letters of the alphabet."[26]

Psalm 119 features twenty-two sections, divided by each successive Hebrew letter—starting with *aleph* and ending with *taw*. Each section contains eight verses. English readers miss out on the alphabetical rhythm deftly woven throughout the psalm, but native Hebrew speakers

Each section of Psalm 119 begins with a letter of the Hebrew alphabet.

כ	י	ט	ח	ז	ו	ה	ד	ג	ב	א
Kaph	Yod	Teth	Heth	Zayin	Waw	Hey	Daleth	Gimel	Beth	Aleph

ת	ש	ר	ק	צ	פ	ע	ס	נ	מ	ל
Taw	Shin	Resh	Kopoh	Tsade	Pey	Ayin	Samek	Nun	Mem	Lamed

would have followed along and anticipated each section while they absorbed attributes of the laws, statutes, and commands of Yahweh. Psalm 119 is the most comprehensive acrostic in the Bible, but it's not the only one. We find acrostics in other psalms, as well as in Proverbs and Lamentations. This invaluable tool helps readers and listeners divide large amounts of information into more accessible sections for memorization and recitation.

Related passages: Psalms 25; 34; 37; 111; 112; 145; Proverbs 31:10–31; Lamentations 4

137:9   Praying for Infanticide?

In Exodus 1:15–21, midwives acted with courageous civil disobedience in the face of a murderous pharaoh who called for the slaughter of Hebrew infants. These women are only one example of the biblical mores concerning Israel's value of children. Yet, in Psalm 137, the psalmist prayed for the specific vengeance of infanticide to be visited upon Babylon.

Sadly, the psalmist's imprecatory prayer described an all-too-typical mode of warfare in the ancient Near East. Referenced in other sections of Scripture, the targeted slaughter of children, pregnant women, and babies was an effective war tactic to ensure that future generations of a nation's enemy would not grow up to exact revenge. In fact, in Isaiah 13:16, the prophet foretold judgment upon Babylon who later would murder the infants of Judah—tying the psalmist's thoughts to the murderous methodology of the Babylonians.

In essence, the psalmist's prayer asked God to remember those who cursed and assaulted His people and to remain true to His promise to protect Abraham's seed. [27]

Related passages: 2 Kings 8:12; Hosea 13:16; Nahum 3:10

PROVERBS

5:4 Bitter Leaves Leave a Bitter Taste

Wormwood, a variety of plant known by the name *Artimisia Absinthium*, grows throughout the land of Israel. It thrives in dry ground and bright sunshine, typically growing to a height of about two feet. The plant's flowers and leafy appearance present a deceptively inviting promise of refreshment for the traveler. Wormwood actually has a strong bitter flavor, which explains why it is associated with bitterness throughout the Bible.

Therefore, Solomon's use of the word *wormwood* in his warning against the adulterous woman stands in stark contrast to the honey that drips from her lips—what appears sweet and good actually brings about a distasteful and revolting result. That the Bible often pairs wormwood with poisonous objects further underlines the negative connotations of this plant.

In Lamentations 3:15, while weeping over a destroyed Jerusalem, Jeremiah explicitly connected wormwood with "bitterness." Interestingly, the word translated "bitterness" is the same word translated "bitter herbs" in Exodus 12:8. This provides a strong possibility that the preparation of the Passover meal included wormwood, which would have made the biblical use of that image that much more potent to a largely Hebrew audience.

Related passages: Deuteronomy 29:18; Jeremiah 9:15; 23:15; Amos 5:7; 6:12; Revelation 8:11

Wells were essential in the ancient world.

5:15   Water Is Life

Wells were essential in the ancient world—especially in a region like Israel with an arid climate. With water often not readily apparent on the surface, people found that they could dig wells to reach underground sources of water. These aquifers offered access to clean drinking water for people and livestock alike.

Much of Israel sits on a layer of limestone, meaning that wells were often dug out of the rock. Sometimes wells featured steps carved around the sides, allowing a person to descend some or all of the way to the water. In other cases, people lowered buckets or animal skins attached to ropes to access the water without having to descend. Wells also regularly had troughs nearby from which livestock could drink.

Due to the paucity of water in this region, wells often became focal points in taking possession of another's land. Therefore, as the people of Israel prepared to enter the Promised Land, Moses reminded them that

God was about to deliver to them many blessings, including cisterns (which stored rainwater) that they did not dig (Deuteronomy 6:11). This sense of proper boundaries factors into the use of the "cistern" and "well" images in Proverbs 5:15, where Solomon compared the life-sustaining power of water to the marriage-sustaining practice of satisfying sexual desires at home with one's spouse, rather than with anyone else.

Related passages: Genesis 29:2; John 4:6

6:1 Secure from Security

Obtaining a loan in the ancient world involved many of the same mechanics it does today. Lenders required security—or surety—from borrowers in order to protect their investments against nonpayment. Garments were among the most common forms of security (Exodus 22:26). Livestock and other items were also common (Genesis 38:17–18).

The most profound form of security one could offer, however, was oneself. Judah offered himself as a guarantee for the safe return of his younger half-brother, Benjamin (43:9), and the psalmist pleaded that the Lord would offer Himself as a guarantee of protection from oppression (Psalm 119:122).

Clearly, offering oneself or one's possessions as security was not out of bounds for God's people. However, because the practice could easily be abused, Solomon offered the wisdom of foresight to those considering offering security for another. Wisdom dictated that God's people not offer surety on behalf of strangers and thereby place themselves in the hands of debtors (Proverbs 6:1). As is true today, this could easily have led to financial ruin and damage to one's standing in the community.

Related passages: Deuteronomy 24:10–13; Proverbs 11:15; 20:16

7:14   A Promise before God

In ancient Israel, a vow, or solemn promise, bound one person to another. Whoever made the vow was expected to follow through with the details the vow prescribed. God did not enjoin His people to make vows. Neither did He pressure them or manipulate them into doing so. If, however, one of God's people (or the whole community of Israel) made a vow, consequences followed if the vow was broken.

With this in mind, Solomon encouraged people to make good on their vows (Ecclesiastes 5:4–6). The expectation that God's people would keep their word to God and to each other, as well as to outsiders, underlined all of this. Although often made by one person to another, all vows were ultimately made before God. In this way, keeping a vow to another person illustrated one's devotion to God.

Fulfilling a vow to God in the biblical era often involved offering a sacrifice (Psalm 56:12). Once the animal was sacrificed, with certain parts of it burnt on the altar and given to the priests, the rest of the meat went home with the one who had offered the sacrifice (Leviticus 7:16–17). [1] Proverbs' adulterous woman's announcement that she had paid her vows "today" was just one more means of enticement—she had fresh meat at home for anyone interested in her company (Proverbs 7:14).

Related passages: 2 Samuel 3:35; Job 22:27; Acts 18:18

14:4   What's in a Manger?

In order to keep livestock from wandering off, ancient people built mangers. Using crisscrossed limbs or stacked stones for walls, farmers and shepherds created these enclosures just large enough for animals to dwell in when they weren't working or grazing. A small gateway inserted into one of the walls allowed the animals to go in and out of the manger.

Such dwelling places would have often been dirty with animal waste. Therefore, when the proverb speaks of a clean manger, it indicates that no animal lived there (Proverbs 14:4); it also suggests something about the work ethic (or lack thereof) of the owner.

The most famous manger in the biblical era sat in Bethlehem, where the holy couple stayed the night Jesus was born because there was no room in the local inn. Scholars today note that the humble setting could have been a traditional manger of stone or wood fences, though many in the early church believed this particular manger was located in a cave. Such a manger had the added benefit of a roof over the heads of the animals, offering extra protection to the farmer's valuable possessions.

Related passages: Job 39:9; Isaiah 1:3; Luke 2:7, 12, 16

16:11   Striking a Balance

Balances played a vital role in the economy of the ancient world. Objects carried certain prices then, just as they do today. These prices were usually represented by weights of precious metals. Therefore, when a person wanted to buy something, he or she brought a small bag of precious metal to the merchant. The merchant attached that bag to one side of a balance or scale via a hook, while the other side held the weight of

Balances and weights were the cash registers of the ancient world.

gold (or something similar) that was needed to purchase the object in question.

Ancient balances were simple and rather crude devices, much like those we have today. A raised crossbeam had a hook affixed to each end. In order for an exchange to take place, the attached buyer's and seller's bags had to render the crossbeam level.

The largest issue in regard to balances involved whether or not a merchant's balances were just—whether or not his weights correctly reflected the agreed upon price. Some shopkeepers added extra weight to their measurements in order to garner more money from their customers. Shoppers and the Lord Himself considered merchants who took advantage of their patrons unjust, something for which He eventually judged His people (Hosea 12:7).

Related passages: Leviticus 19:36; Proverbs 11:1; Ezekiel 45:10

18:10–11   Protection from Enemies

Ancient peoples needed places of strength from which to withstand attacks from hostile neighbors or invaders. One of the most common defensive structures, a strong or fortified tower made primarily of stone, could hold both people and supplies. Further, it gave defenders a high perch from which to do battle, a position that is preferable in a military conflict.

Towers could be stand-alone defenses both outside and inside cities, but they could also be incorporated into fortified cities, buttressed on either side by walls as wide as six feet thick. These walls surrounded the cities with gates every so often to provide access. Some cities even incorporated a moat around the outside of the walls to provide one more level of fortification. Biblical writers often used this potent image as a stand-in for God's protection and power.

Towers, walls, and other such defenses that surrounded many ancient cities were the only protection for the people who lived in and

Walls like this one in Jerusalem provided ancient cities with their strongest defense.

around urban centers. Attacks upon such fortified cities would have been especially difficult and drawn out, requiring lengthy and costly sieges to starve out the inhabitants and/or coordinated attacks to scale or breach the walls. That fact makes the battle at Jericho all the more impressive for its swift resolution (Joshua 6:20).

Related passages: Judges 9:51; Proverbs 18:19; Isaiah 26:1

18:18   Divining the Will of God

In ancient times, people cast lots to determine what God wanted them to do, a practice supported by the Mosaic Law itself (Leviticus 16:8). Scripture refers to the event often, but it never describes the exact process or materials used. Many have suggested that the "lots" were actually marked stones. The "caster" would gather the stones in a small cup, cover it with his hand, and cast out a single stone that would help him answer the question at hand. Ancient Israelites saw this as a reliable way to make decisions without the selfishness or bias of human beings.

People cast lots for many reasons, including: dividing land (Numbers 33:54), choosing an army (Judges 20:8–9), and answering disputed questions (Proverbs 16:33). The most famous moment of lot-casting in human history is likely the one associated with the crucifixion, when the guards cast lots for Jesus' robe (John 19:23–24). People also relied on lots to appoint people to special offices such as priest (Luke 1:9) and apostle (Acts 1:26). Worth noting, the practice never appears again by God's people after the coming of the Holy Spirit in Acts 2.

Related passages: Joshua 18:6; 1 Chronicles 24:31

21:9   Roofing It

Even more than architecture does today, ancient construction gave emphasis to the usage of built spaces, not just to their style. To that end, builders constructed homes from a variety of designs, creating places where inhabitants could perform and meet a number of tasks and needs.

Most homes in the ancient Near East had flat roofs, which allowed people to use them for additional activities. People's roofs doubled as

A rooftop view of Jerusalem

storage space for their excess produce, out of the way of normal, day-to-day life. Psalm 129:6 notes the presence of grass growing upon housetops. And Proverbs 21:9 suggests that people could live at the corners of their roofs. The flatness of the space made this possible, though the proverb refers to living on the roof in a negative sense—as a means for a man to avoid a contentious woman!

Deuteronomy 22:8 made building walls around roofs the standard for God's people. If a roof was used for socializing and for sleeping at night in the warm summer months (1 Samuel 9:25–26), a parapet around the edges would have been a great advantage.

Related passages: Joshua 2:6; Acts 10:9

24:30–31   Strong Wall, Strong Worker

Walls of stone often bordered vineyards and farming fields in the ancient world. Farmers understood the importance of keeping crops separate from one another. Cross-growth could threaten the purity and the survival of certain crops.

Creating a stone wall around a plot of farmland involved piling stones atop one another, placing large stones on the bottom and smaller stones on top and in the holes where uneven stones came together. Animals, invaders, or even weather could topple walls constructed in such a simple fashion. Therefore, stone walls needed regular maintenance in order to continue to fulfill their purposes of separating one section of land from another and of protecting the crop within their enclosures.

Stone walls also served a purpose within enclosures on hillsides. Typically, hillside farmers terraced their land, creating several flat spaces to grow their crops. A short stone wall supported each terrace. If these stone walls weren't maintained, the entire crop could come to ruin.

Related passages: Numbers 22:24; Isaiah 5:5; Matthew 21:33

ECCLESIASTES

2:5   The King's Garden

In an area that may otherwise have been ignored, the City of David—the original city of Jerusalem—had an abundant water supply that flowed seemingly out of nowhere, allowing King Solomon to ambitiously cultivate royal parks and gardens.

During Solomon's reign, as today, the Kidron Valley lay on the eastern side of Jerusalem. Waters cut through the limestone, creating karstic waterways underground that gushed up, forming the Gihon Spring, the main water source for the city. Ancient city planners previously had carved these natural waterways to their advantage, creating a system now referred to as Warren's Shaft.

The Gihon Spring played a critical role in supplying water to the city during military sieges. During times of peace, it was the main irrigation source for the king's gardens (2 Kings 25:4; Nehemiah 3:15; Jeremiah 52:7).

> The spring emerged in a cave on the eastern slope of the City of David above the Kidron Valley, and from there water flowed into the valley, watering the terraced, agricultural plots on the slope of the City of David. This area is called in the Bible the "King's Garden."[1]

Solomon's gardens and parks were incredible feats of agriculture, so much so that Solomon used a Persian loanword, *pardes*, to describe them. *Pardes* defined the exclusive opulence of royal grounds and led to the English word "paradise."[2]

2:7   Homeborn Slaves

Solomon's expansive kingdom was unparalleled in affluence and bounty and, as such, necessitated a fleet of guards, farmers, landscapers, stable hands, cooks, maids, soldiers, and a host of other positions. Some positions were filled with servants and volunteers, but there were also slaves in Solomon's kingdom. In Ecclesiastes 2:7, Solomon referenced "homeborn" slaves, those who were slaves from birth due to their parents' enslaved status.

Curiously, the Old Testament does not explicitly condemn slavery. Rather, it declares that the people of God were to be peculiar—which is to say, humane—in dealing with slaves. Typically, slaves were acquired through warfare when the defeated parties were enslaved to the victors or through indebtedness whereby a person paid off his or her debt through servitude. Unlike the chattel slavery of the Atlantic slave trade, which stripped the enslaved of any form of human dignity or hope for freedom, slaves in the ancient Near East had a right to own property—even other slaves—as well as rights to conduct business. [3] In the kingdom of Israel, homeborn slaves—and their enslaved parents—could earn their freedom. And at the Year of Jubilee, all slaves were to be set free.

Related passages: Genesis 15:3; 17:12–13, 27; Leviticus 25:47–55; Jeremiah 2:14

10:10   The Axe Is Dull

Ecclesiastes 10 begins with a theme of practical advice for personal peace and moves into the realm of occupational hazards in verse 8. Each of Solomon's hazard examples serves a dual purpose: to pragmatically improve safety and effectiveness and, through metaphor, to encourage wise living. Ecclesiastes 10:10 teaches that a sharpened axe is more effective, cutting the user's time and exertion.

Before the Israelites learned ironwork from the Philistines (1 Samuel 13:19), their axes were made of stone, copper, or bronze. By Solomon's day, an axe was as common to a household as a Swiss army knife is today—an everyday, practical essential. In fact, the axe was such

A sharp axe can cut a user's time and effort.

a common tool that *seven* different Hebrew words are translated as "axe" in English translations of the Bible. In this instance, the word *axe* comes from the Hebrew word for "iron," *barzel*, instead of the more common Hebrew term, *garzen*—which comes from the root word that means "to sever."[4] Solomon's choice in words emphasized the reason why an axe needed maintenance: iron must be sharpened in order to be effective.

Related passages: Deuteronomy 19:5; 2 Samuel 12:31; 2 Kings 6:5–6; 1 Chronicles 20:3

11:1 A Soggy Mess?

Scholars fall into two different camps when translating and interpreting Ecclesiastes 11:1. The first camp, the more popular one, translates the verse as, "Cast your bread on the surface of the waters, for you will find it after many days" (NASB, KJV). This interpretation views "casting of bread" as acts of charity toward others (MSG). The translation emphasizes that generosity is a worthy cause, and spreading one's fortune through giving is wise, because tomorrow is not promised (Ecclesiastes 11:2). Several other English Bible versions choose a translation that gives readers a completely different interpretation: "Send your grain overseas, for after many days you will get a return" (NET, see also NIV, NLT). In this interpretation, "sending grain" signifies overseas commerce. In the ancient Near East, maritime commerce was prone to destruction or piracy and, therefore, viewed as a high-risk venture. However, this risky form of trade often produced much higher dividends. In the context of chapter 11, which highlights the virtue of prudence and diligence, a business advice interpretation makes sense. [5]

Related passages: 1 Kings 9:26–28; 10:22; Psalm 107:23

11:6 Sowing Diligently

The first audiences and authors of the Old Testament lived in agrarian communities. As a result, farming terminology is ubiquitous in Scripture. Sowing—the scattering of seed for the purpose of planting crops—could not be done half-heartedly if the farmer wanted to reap a bountiful harvest. Variables like rain, drought, extreme heat, and foraging animals all took a toll on how great a crop a farmer could reap. In addition, the soil varied greatly in areas of Israel—the coastal plains were fertile all year around, while the hill country was better for grazing.[6] One aspect a farmer *could* control, however, was the work he accomplished between "morning" and "evening"—the all-day diligence of planting seeds. That kind of dedication almost guaranteed a bumper crop.

Biblical writers commonly incorporated agricultural terms like *sowing* and *reaping* in the Bible as metaphors depicting the consistent, dedicated work involved in spiritual and emotional investment and return. Jesus' parable of the soils in the New Testament is one example, and it would have made perfect sense to listeners quite familiar with how soil quality affects successful sowing (Mark 4:3–9).

Related passages: Exodus 23:10; Leviticus 25:3–4; Job 4:8; Psalm 97:11; 126:5; Proverbs 11:18; 22:8; Ecclesiastes 11:4; Isaiah 30:23; 61:11; Jeremiah 31:27; Hosea 2:23; 8:7; Matthew 6:26; 13:3–9; Luke 8:5–8; John 4:36–37; 1 Corinthians 15:36–44; 2 Corinthians 9:6; Galatians 6:7–8; James 3:18

SONG OF SOLOMON

1:3 Sweet-Smelling Oils

Ancient people improved their odor by applying sweet-smelling oils to their bodies. The best oil for such purposes came from olives, which were especially common in ancient Israel. However, scented oils were decidedly uncommon and a sign of a person's wealth or prominence. That the woman of Song of Solomon compared her lover's name to perfume suggests that she held him in very high regard. His "name" was his reputation.

The process of pressing standard olive oil began with olives and a large millstone. Farmers piled the olives in a circular stone trough; then a horse pulled the millstone around the trough. Oil from the crushed olives seeped out a hole near the top of the trough. Farmers then carefully pressed the olive pulp, draining the remains of the oil to yield the largest amount.

To achieve the purified oil (or cologne/perfume) that appears in Song of Solomon 1:3, standard olive oil was combined with various spices such as cinnamon, myrrh, cane, and cassia (Exodus 30:22–25). The exact method of getting the spices into the oil is unknown, though they may have been boiled in water before being combined with the oil in order to create the perfumed mixture.

Related passages: Ecclesiastes 7:1; 10:1; Song of Solomon 4:10

A mare was a symbol of beauty and rarity.

1:9   Mare-y Me!

A mare (or female horse) among Pharaoh's chariots would have been a unique incident indeed. In general, pairs of stallions (or male horses) pulled ancient chariots, and the stallions of Pharaoh's army would have been among the best and strongest in the world. To have sent a mare in among them would likely have incited a riotous scene as the virile horses pursued the lone female in their midst.

Furthermore, horses were not at all common in the ancient world in and around Israel. The animals weren't native to the immediate region; thus, they would have had to be imported into the country. Therefore, horses belonged only to the wealthiest and most powerful people. Solomon spoke of his beloved as a mare among Pharaoh's best stallions not simply to highlight her attractiveness but also her rarity and value.

Israel had few horses, in large part, because Mosaic Law rejected breeding them or even importing them, likely so God's people would avoid relying on powerful armies as their strength (Deuteronomy 17:16). That David captured and Solomon eventually imported large numbers of horses suggests that national defense, at least in those cases, was more important to the rulers than obedience to God's Law (2 Samuel 8:3–4; 2 Chronicles 1:16).

Related passages: Psalm 33:17–18; Jeremiah 47:3

2:15   Be on the Alert for Foxes

The ancients thought of the fox in much the same way we do today: as a crafty animal that can cause great harm to livestock and crops—sources of many people's livelihoods. These animals live solitary lives, burrowing homes underground and seeking out fruit, small rodents, and poultry for sustenance.

The craftiness of the fox—sneaking around where it's not welcome in order to find food—is its most striking characteristic. Song of Solomon 2:15 emphasizes the destructive power of such craftiness. Here, the couple in love call out for others to help them watch out for metaphorical foxes—anyone or anything that might bring ruin to their budding relationship.

Foxes make unsavory appearances throughout Scripture. In Luke 13:32, Jesus spoke of Herod as a fox when He heard that the latter was seeking to take His life. Jesus' use of this image suggests a very negative evaluation of foxes in ancient Israel—one that had long been in place. In the period of the judges, Samson brought down punishment upon the Philistines by capturing foxes, tying torches to their tails, and setting the lit foxes loose among the Philistine crops (Judges 15:4–5). Unlike today, no one would have complained about foxes—dangerous pests—being used for such purposes.

Related passages: Lamentations 5:18; Ezekiel 13:4; Matthew 8:20

8:1   Hey, Brother!

Just as they can today, sibling relationships in the ancient world could be sources of great reward and also great pain. Growing up in close proximity offered the chance to develop rich and lasting relationships but also provided ample opportunity to frustrate and hurt each other deeply. The book of Proverbs reveals this dual nature of sibling relationships, both presuming the natural closeness of a sibling (Proverbs 18:24) and suggesting the difficulties of being in a sibling relationship (17:17). The positives and negatives of sibling relationships come out in surprising ways in Scripture. On the one hand, by asking his wife to pretend to be his sister, Abraham used the false cover of a close sibling relationship to protect his interests in foreign territory (Genesis 12:13). But Scripture also reveals Amnon abusing that sibling intimacy by raping his half-sister, Tamar (2 Samuel 13:1).

The sibling imagery in Song of Solomon shows this dual nature in more explicit fashion. Ancient Middle Eastern culture believed it inappropriate for men and women who weren't blood relations to embrace and kiss in public. Thus, the female in Song of Solomon wished her lover were her brother so she could kiss him without judgment (Song of Solomon 8:1). However, earlier in the book, we also see her frustration with her actual brothers when they made her work outside, leading to her skin being damaged by the sun (1:6).

Related passages: Genesis 25:26; 37:4

8:9   Strong Walls and Swinging Doors

Solomon evoked two different ancient structures in Song of Solomon chapter 8: city walls and common household doors. City walls were generally fashioned by stacking bricks on top of one another. Bricks were usually made of clay combined with straw or reed but could also be fashioned from stone. The latter process involved carving the bricks out of rock and dragging the heavy pieces to wherever the people were building a wall. Song of Solomon 8:9 mentions covering the wall with a

Battlements in the Tower of David area of Jerusalem

silver battlement—a series of metal stones along the top of the wall that strengthened the defense and made it more beautiful. In this context, a woman as a "wall" represented her morality as she resisted anyone entering.

Homes have always needed access points, and doors were common in the ancient Near East as they are today. Doors were usually made of wood or stone. Wood doors might also have been covered with metal to strengthen and preserve the wood beneath. As they do today, people often decorated their doors with precious metals or carvings, giving personality to the entrance of their homes. Doors generally hung on hinges (Proverbs 26:14) but were also sometimes mounted on rollers. People secured their doors with large bars or locks (Judges 3:23; 16:3). Song of Solomon 8:9 speaks of barricading a door with cedar to prevent the door from opening. In this context, a woman who was a "door" was an immoral person who allowed access when it wasn't appropriate.

Related passage: Song of Solomon 5:5

ISAIAH

1:8   Watchman's Hut

Much of the Western world is unfamiliar with the rhythms of farming.
Not so with Isaiah's audience, who could've easily recalled visions of
lonely, reaped fields sparsely dotted with empty lean-tos. Near harvest
time in the ancient Near East, fields were especially vulnerable to thieves
and wild animals. During this season, watchmen inhabited makeshift
shelters in the fields in order to work as security guards. After the harvest, the need for security diminished, and the shelters stood abandoned.
Because guarding fields was a temporary task, watchmen's huts and
vineyard shelters were characterized by rickety frames. These ramshackle
buildings, porous and susceptible, could not withstand any significant
weather or long-term habitation. After the harvest, without the presence
of the watchmen, the shelters quickly fell prey to their environments.
Isaiah drew upon this image when he observed that Jerusalem, without
the Lord's protection, found itself desolate and vulnerable, like a vineyard
shelter, abandoned and open to military attack. [1]

2:12   What Is the "Day of the Lord"?

Throughout the prophetic books of the Bible, the "Day of the
Lord"—also referenced as "that day" or "the day"—describes a day of
reckoning for idolatrous kingdoms, especially those who were callous
toward God's people, the Israelites. For example, the prophet Isaiah
wrote of Babylon's comeuppance at the hands of the Medes (Isaiah 13).
God's judgment, however, extended not only to foreign nations. Isaiah
warned Israel that its idolatry had placed it squarely in the crosshairs of
Yahweh's wrath. Isaiah, along with Ezekiel and Amos, described "The
Day" of discipline for God's people through foreign occupation and exile

(Isaiah 13; Ezekiel 13:5; Amos 5–6). Mercifully, through Joel, Yahweh promised to save a faithful remnant (Joel 2:28–32). [2]

In light of the incarnation of Jesus Christ, the New Testament expounds on the idea of reckoning, describing an ultimate Day of the Lord, which will usher in Christ's second coming (1 Corinthians 1:8, 5:5). Peter described the conclusion of the Day as having "intense heat" and noted that "the earth and its works will be burned up" (2 Peter 3:10). At the end of the Day of the Lord, all sin will be reckoned with, and true worshipers will be rewarded with God's eternal presence.

Related passages: Jeremiah 46:10; Joel 1:15; 2:1, 11, 31; 3:14; Obadiah 15; Zephaniah 1:7, 14; Zechariah 14:1; Philippians 1:6, 10; 2:16; 2 Thessalonians 2:2

3:18–23 Tinkle, Tinkle, Little Bangle

In Isaiah's day, the women of Zion succumbed to the temptation to fix their value upon their possessions rather than their God. The prophet,

Superstitious ancient Near Easterners would sometimes wear "evil eye" talismans like these to ward off evil.

therefore, laid out a laundry list of adornments that would be removed from them. To indicate the full measure of His discipline, Yahweh, through Isaiah, went down the line of women's ornaments, progressing from the nonessential and decorative to the bare necessities that indicated femininity and ensured modesty:

Crescent ornaments, found to this day, were necklaces to ward off the "evil eye." Such cultic talismans had no place on a woman of Zion.

Bracelets, worn by both men and women, served as status symbols in many ancient Near Eastern cultures. Royal women wore their bracelets above the elbow, while common folks wore them at the wrist.

Outer tunics, cloaks, money purses, undergarments, and turbans were necessities for women of every class. Stripping them of these practical garments meant certain shame and nakedness—conditions befitting a slave.

Veils indicated the marital status of a woman (Genesis 24:65)—only unmarried women donned veils.

The superiority of beautifying from the inside out through devotion to God rather than external baubles persisted through the Old Testament to the New. The apostles Paul and Peter expounded on the idea in their letters (1 Timothy 2:9–10; 1 Peter 3:3–4), and the prescription for inner beauty to eclipse outer adornment continues to this day.

Related passages: Genesis 24:22, 30; Judges 8:21; 2 Samuel 1:24; Song of Solomon 1:10; Jeremiah 2:32; Ezekiel 16:11–12

6:2 Seraphim: The Burning Ones

Seraphim are literally the "burning ones," angelic servants of Yahweh, created to extol the holiness of God. Interestingly, the Hebrew word *seraphim* sometimes refers to "fiery serpents" (Numbers 21:6, 8), perhaps because a snake's poisonous venom and stinging bite tends to "burn" its victims. Though some Baroque and Renaissance painters depicted *seraphim* differently, these angels were far from chubby, placid, winged babies or androgynous figures clad in diaphanous garb. These special ministers are stationed closest to God's throne and are tasked with constantly declaring His holiness (Isaiah 6:2–3; Revelation 4:8). Some believe that the *seraphim* described in the book of Isaiah are analogous with the *cherubim* described in Ezekiel 1 and 10 but are differently labeled in order to distinguish how they specifically functioned in each passage (i.e., when they worshiped at God's throne as opposed to when they guarded His holiness from man's defilement, as in Genesis 3:24). [3]

Related passages: Deuteronomy 8:15; Isaiah 6:6–7; 14:29; Ezekiel 1:5–25

6:13   O Terebinth Tree, O Terebinth Tree

Bible translators often translate the Hebrew word *elah* as "terebinth" tree or "oak" tree (Genesis 35:4). [4] The terebinth is a type of tree that produces nuts similar in form and flavor to the pistachio. An expansive plant with arching branches and leaves, a terebinth tree can grow to twenty-five feet in height and bloom with red berries and bright crimson foliage. However, biblically speaking, the terebinth wasn't renowned for its stunning appearance or ability to produce food. Rather, the terebinth's religious significance set it apart. Terebinth trees commonly served as canopies for both sacred and idolatrous activity. In Judges 6, Gideon entertained an angel at a terebinth tree, while in Hosea 4, Israel chose a terebinth as a location to "play the harlot" by worshiping false gods. In Isaiah 6:13, the stump of the terebinth cradled a "holy seed" that cannot be burned or felled.

Related passages: Joshua 24:26; Judges 6:11, 19; Isaiah 1:30; Hosea 4:13

7:15   Curds and Honey

When ancient Near Easterners heard the phrase, "curds and honey," they knew immediately that whoever partook of that particular snack lived in the Land of Promise and participated in the peaceful blessing of the

Milk curds and honey

land's yield. Soft, sweet, plentiful, and easy-to-eat, curds and honey were common first foods for ancient Israelite children—those who didn't yet "know enough to refuse evil and choose good" (Isaiah 7:15). Curds, also translated as "sour milk" or "butter," were traditionally made from the milk of camels, goats, or cows. "Honey" was either the nectar of bees or syrup made from dates. Both milk and honey were abundant in ancient Israel, even during lean times—a reminder of God's promise to take His people into a land of provision, one "flowing with milk and honey" (Exodus 3:17).

In an ironic twist, Isaiah said that these foods that symbolized abundant provision would eventually become Israel's quintessential food to get by—the food they would eat when they had very little, similar to cornmeal porridge in Jamaica or ramen noodles in college circles today. After Assyria's dreadful coming occupation, Israel, the prophet declared, would eat curds and honey out of scarcity, not plenty, because these would be the only foods left (Isaiah 7:20–25).[5]

Related passage: Numbers 13:17–27

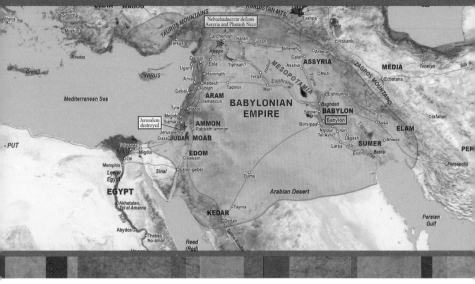

Map of regions mentioned in Isaiah 21
Map from *Satellite Bible Atlas.* Copyright © 2012 by William Schlegel. All rights reserved worldwide. Used by permission.

21:1 "The Wilderness of the Sea" and Other Obscure Places

Simply put, the "wilderness of the sea" or "desert of the sea" (Isaiah 21:1 NIV, KJV) means "**Babylon**." The prophet Isaiah used the title to address the empire with irony. Babylon, at that time, had yet to ascend to the fullness of its power, but it was still cradled by the Euphrates River and flourishing—far from a wilderness. But, Isaiah portended, Babylon's destruction would render it desolate.

After addressing Babylon, the prophet also spoke of the following now little-known nations:

Elam and **Media**: Babylon's eastern neighbor, Elam—the name of a son of Shem (Genesis 10:22)—and northern neighbor, Media, would suffer under Babylon's rule and, therefore, eagerly desire emancipation.

Edom/Seir: Edom, meaning "red," is associated with Esau, his tribe, and his land (Genesis 25:30). Throughout the Bible, Edom represents opposition to the chosen people of Israel. Mount Seir is in the land of Edom.

Arabia/Dedanites: Arabia, of which Dedan was a city, is thought to be located in modern-day Saudi Arabia. Arabians/Dedanites were known for their caravan trade and nomadic lifestyle. [6]

Kedar: Originally one of the sons of Ishmael (Genesis 25:13), the name Kedar eventually became synonymous with foreign distance. The nation Kedar was renowned for its tents (Psalm 120:5; Song of Solomon 1:5) and herds (Isaiah 60:7; Ezekiel 27:21).

Related passages: Numbers 20:14–21; Isaiah 29:7

29:1–2   More Than Just a Mermaid

Long before Disney adapted Hans Christian Andersen's dark fairy tale *The Little Mermaid* into a musical cartoon with a redheaded mermaid and a famous singing shellfish, there was Ariel. In Hebrew, *Ariel* means "hearth of God," and the term found its brilliance in its ability to evoke multiple connotations. [7] In ancient Israel, the hearth was the center of every home, essential because it was the place where fire was kindled, for warmth or for cooking. [8] The prophet Ezekiel, in the Hebrew text, called upon this idea when he referred to the temple altar hearth as "Ariel" (Ezekiel 43:15–16). However, *Ariel* did not always conjure warm images. Isaiah used the term to warn Jerusalem of the fiery fate they would endure if they did not put an end to their idolatry. In one sense, Jerusalem was the "hearth of God" because it was the heart of Israel, the nation with whom He chose to dwell. But in a terribly foreboding sense, Jerusalem, God warned, would quite literally become His hearth, singed by fire if they continued to divide their hearts.

Related passage: Isaiah 29:7

46:1   Who Are Bel and Nebo?

Bel—also referred to as Maraduch or Marduk [9]—was king of the gods, according to the Enuma Elish, Babylon's creation myth. [10] The power of Bel signified Babylon's power. Nebo, or Nabu, was the son of Bel. The Babylonians considered Nebo the god of learning, especially in the sciences, astronomy, and writing.[11] Kings garnered authority in part through invoking these gods in their names: *Bel*teshazzar or *Nebu*chadnezzar, for example. Further, Bel could have been the image that Nebuchadnezzar required his subjects to worship in Daniel 3.

Together, the two gods represented the massive power and intellect of Babylon. Yahweh implored the people of Israel to remember that He alone is God, knowing that they were attracted to the power of Babylon, and by extension, Babylon's false gods. That Bel and Nebo were the father-son duo that the Babylonians and unfaithful Israelites worshiped makes their contrast to Yahweh in the book of Isaiah all the more pointed—Yahweh and His Servant are the *real* Father-Son duo worthy of worship.

Related passages: Jeremiah 50:2; 51:44

62:3   Diadems

Both the Old and New Testaments are fraught with references to "crowns." For example, the "crown of the head," *qodqod* in Hebrew, is often used in the Old Testament as a synonym for "the top of the head"

The diadem of Princess Sit-Hathor Yunet, daughter of Pharaoh, Senusret II

(Genesis 49:26; Deuteronomy 28:36; 2 Samuel 14:25; Psalm 68:21). In Exodus, the Hebrew word *nezer*, or "holy crown," communicates a sense of consecration (Exodus 29:6). Then there's the New Testament crown of achievement mentioned in many of the epistles (1 Corinthians 9:25; 2 Timothy 4:8; 1 Peter 5:4).

In Isaiah 62:3, the *diadem* — *'atarah* in Hebrew — is distinguished as the adornment for one given the right to rule. The headgear of bona fide royalty, a diadem could be a crown made of precious metal or even a turban. Isaiah referenced the diadem earlier in the book, comparing the Lord of Hosts to a glorious diadem crowning the righteous remnant. In Isaiah 62, Zion — the land symbolizing the righteous remnant — is given the diadem befitting a bridal queen.

The book of Revelation affirms Isaiah's prophecy, asserting Jesus' right to rule with crown imagery (Revelation 19:12). Not all diadems, however, are rightly given. Satan, the imposter, is also depicted wearing many diadems in Revelation 12:3 and 13:1.

Related passages: 2 Kings 11:12; Isaiah 28:5

JEREMIAH

―❦―

2:13   Choosing Cisterns

In the ancient Near East in Jeremiah's time, "living water"—natural
springs of fresh water—constituted the best and most reliable source
of water. God gave His people a land with a variety of sources of water
(Deuteronomy 8:7). The Gihon Spring flowed near Jerusalem and
provided fresh water (2 Chronicles 32:30). Because spring water flowed
continually, it was clean and refreshing. For those who didn't live near
springs, cisterns were another source of water. These pear-shaped holes
dug in the ground and covered with plaster caught rainwater. Because
they depended on rainfall, cisterns didn't provide consistent water; they
also often cracked and leaked. The collected water sat stagnant and
contained dirt, leaves, and other debris carried by the wind. Cisterns that
would no longer hold water were sometimes used as prisons.

God spoke through Jeremiah to chastise His people for choosing
idols over Him, the Lord of all creation. In Him, they had reliable, fresh-
flowing, satisfying "living water"—spiritual water that would never run
dry. Yet they chose idols that were like broken cisterns that couldn't even
provide dirty, unreliable water. [1]

Related passage: Jeremiah 38:6

2:16   Ancient Haircuts

In Jeremiah's day, the Lord allowed His people, who had abandoned Him, to fall into the hands of Memphis and Tahpanhes, two influential cities in Egypt. The Lord spoke through Jeremiah, saying the Egyptians had "shaved the crown of [His people's] head." The reference most likely refers to when Pharaoh Neco killed Josiah, Judah's king (or "crown"), at Megiddo in 609 BC (2 Kings 23:29 – 30).[2] Although Neco may not have literally shaved Josiah's head, the wording would've been potent to Hebrew ears. The Hebrews viewed every part of their bodies, including their hair, as belonging to God. Cutting or shaving off all of one's hair, except in the case of mourning or purification after leprosy, was highly unorthodox. Occasional trims were okay for priests, for example, so that their hair wouldn't get in the way of their duties (Ezekiel 44:20). In Egypt and other ancient Near Eastern nations, however, men often shaved their hair as part of pagan religious rituals.[3] When God's people aligned themselves with Egypt or other pagan nations, they may have also adopted their pagan rituals, including haircutting. God, however, wanted His people, and their haircuts, to be unique and separate from the nations.

Related passages: 2 Samuel 14:26; Jeremiah 25:22–24; 49:32

4:5   Shofar, So Good

Jeremiah told the Israelites who lived in Judah to blow the trumpet, gather in fortified cities, and take cover because the enemy from the north would soon attack. Ancient Israelites signaled a coming invasion with a trumpet known as a shofar. Seven times in his book, Jeremiah mentioned the sound of the shofar and its signal of war and judgment. Israelites used the shofar, a wind instrument made from a ram's horn, for more than just warning citizens of an impending attack (Jeremiah 4:19, 21). God's people blew the shofar to signal the Year of Jubilee, the new moon feast day, and joyful worship. To this day, rabbis

The shofar is a wind instrument made from a ram's horn.

blow the shofar at religious holidays and each Friday evening to signal the beginning of Sabbath.

Related passages: Leviticus 25:9–10; Psalm 81:3; 98:6

7:18   Does Heaven Have a Queen?

The Queen of Heaven cult, dedicated to Astarte (or Ishtar), the Assyrian-Babylonian goddess of love and fertility, plagued God's people for years. In this cult, worshipers made drink offerings and sacrifices of special cakes shaped like Astarte or the moon. This goddess was symbolized by astral bodies such as a moon, Venus, or a star. Women who participated in this cult prepared the cakes. The fact that the people considered this goddess the "queen" points to her preeminent role above other goddesses.

When Manasseh ruled Judah (697–642 BC) and the Queen of Heaven cult started to take hold, God promised to judge His people (2 Kings 21:10–17). Even during the religious reforms of Josiah, which began in 628 BC, people continued to worship Asherah (probably another name for Astarte) at shrines set up in their homes (23:4–14). By the time of Jeremiah's ministry (627–587 BC), the abominable Queen of Heaven cult had so infiltrated Judah's culture that entire families, including children, came together to prepare offerings and participate in cult worship. [4] God had finally had enough, and He came through on His promise to mete out judgment in 586 BC when King Nebuchadnezzar of Babylon destroyed Jerusalem. Jeremiah called God's people to repentance, but they refused and promised to continue their idolatrous rituals (Jeremiah 44:15–19).

Related passage: Jeremiah 7:19–20

9:17   Mourners for Hire

In the Old Testament, mourning took place following a death, tragedy, sin, or God's judgment. When people faced such occasions, they often hired "mourning women," or professional mourners, to help them voice their grief. These women accompanied funeral parties and cried out in high-pitched wails. Egyptian art found in ancient tombs depicts such professional mourners. To this day in the Middle East, grief-stricken individuals can hire professional mourners for funerals or for grieving tragedies.

The Bible speaks of different methods of mourning: weeping, lamentation, and personal disfigurement. Weeping was grief-inspired crying (Genesis 23:2). Lamentation often included loud wailing and shrieking such as when the firstborn in Egypt died, in approximately 1446 BC (Exodus 12:30). After Israel died, the Egyptians mourned for him for seventy days. Mourners frequently disfigured themselves by tearing their clothing, wearing sackcloth, sprinkling dust on themselves, fasting, or cutting their hair (Job 1:20). "Mourning women" likely employed all these methods. [5]

Related passage: Genesis 50:3

22:24   Signed and Sealed

A signet bore a certain design and carried the same authority as a king's signature. Egyptians started using signets made of porcelain or pottery as early as c. 2550 BC. As far back as c. 3500 BC, the Mesopotamians had created small cylindrical signets that could leave an official impression when rolled over moist clay. [6] Hebrew kings used their signets in this way (Job 38:14) and often wore their signet rings on strings around their necks or on their arms (Song of Solomon 8:6).

An ancient Near Eastern king didn't easily part with his signet ring. With his signet ring, a king signed statutes into law, sealed people's fates (Daniel 6:17), and displayed his authority. But even if evil King Coniah (Jehoiachin) of Judah had been God's signet ring, in His wrath, the Lord would have ripped Coniah off and thrown him away. Abusing his authority, King Coniah had followed in his father's sinful footsteps and led God's people to forsake Him (2 Kings 24:9).

Related passages: Esther 3:10 – 12; 8:2 – 10

Kings pressed their signet rings into moist clay to seal important documents.

A modern-day replica of a papyrus roll

36:4   Scribes and Scrolls

Like many scribes in his day, Jeremiah's scribe, Baruch, probably wrote on papyrus scrolls with pen and ink (Jeremiah 8:8). Some scribes might have used iron styluses (17:1), but Baruch and many others likely used pens made of coarse grass and cut diagonally with a scribe's knife. They dipped their pens in ink made of soot or lampblack and gum mixed with water. In Jeremiah 36, when King Jehoiakim had had enough of hearing Jehudi speak God's condemning words that Jeremiah's scribe had recorded, the king used a scribe's knife to cut up the scroll (36:23).

When scribes finished writing or compiling words on a certain topic, the resulting works were called "books," such as the books of the Law (Joshua 23:6). Scribes used papyrus scrolls to record historical, religious, and other works until the time when the New Testament writers began recording God's words. Archaeologists have found scrolls with portions of the Greek New Testament dating back to the second century AD that show how reliable our copies of Scripture are today. However, starting around the time of the New Testament, literary works began being compiled on single sheets and bound in books or codices. By the third century in Egypt, the codex had almost replaced the scroll, at least in the copying of New Testament Scripture. [7]

Related passages: Isaiah 30:8; Hebrews 10:7

37:15   Behind Bars

When Jeremiah warned King Zedekiah that the Babylonian army would surely destroy Jerusalem, the captain of the king's guard arrested the prophet for treason with a sentence of prison (Jeremiah 37:1–16). After enduring a beating by the king's officials, Jeremiah entered prison in the house of Jonathan the scribe. Jeremiah's cell was either part of a large complex of cisterns converted into prison cells or a vaulted cell within a dungeon. [8] The prophet feared for his life there (37:20). Earlier in his ministry, Jeremiah had been held in the court of the guard, a heavily guarded area located in the king's palace complex, where Jeremiah received visitors and purchased a field (32:2, 8, 12). Within this court was a cistern, into which the guards threw Jeremiah when they wearied of hearing God's words (38:2–6). Because they were difficult to escape from, abandoned cisterns were often turned into prison cells.

Several others in the Old Testament experienced time in prison. Joseph was held in the palace prison over which Potiphar, captain of Pharaoh's bodyguard, ruled (Genesis 39:19–22). Some prisoners survived on bread and water (1 Kings 22:27), wore prison clothes (2 Kings 25:29), and were held in stocks (Jeremiah 20:2).

Related passage: 2 Chronicles 18:26

43:13   Obliterating Obelisks

Made with four sides and topped with a pyramid shape, obelisks were tall monuments often built for the sun god, Amon-Re. Occasionally, they also commemorated important historical events. When the inhabitants of Judah disobeyed God and fled to Egypt, they arrived in the city of On, about ten miles northeast of modern-day Cairo. As a center of worship for the sun god Amon-Re, On had earned the nickname "Heliopolis" or "sun city." With a pantheon of gods to choose from, Egyptians bowed down to a number of gods they connected to weather and natural phenomena to ensure agricultural success. Their livelihoods depended on the sun to produce good crops. In Heliopolis, worshipers set up two rows of obelisks outside the temple of Amon-Re as a part of their religious rituals. One of these obelisks still stands on site today, and another stands in Rome at St. John Lateran. [9]

God pursued His people to Egypt and, through the hand of King Nebuchadnezzar of Babylon, chastened them and obliterated the obelisks where they had violated His first commandment (Jeremiah 43:13).

Related passage: Jeremiah 42:9–19

Luxor Obelisk in Place de la Concorde in Paris

47:1   Ancient Gaza

Located about fifty miles southwest of Jerusalem, Gaza was an important city on trade and military routes from Egypt to Israel, Syria, and other Mesopotamian nations. As military campaigns traveled the route that passed through Gaza, they often took over and established their power in each city, including Gaza, before marching on to their ultimate destinations.

Gaza makes its first biblical appearance in Genesis 10:19 as a prominent city in the land of the Philistines. Throughout history, Israel battled the Philistines, who regularly tried to expand their territory. When God gave His people the Promised Land, Joshua conquered most of the Philistines' land, including Gaza (Joshua 10:41). When Joshua divided the conquered land between the twelve tribes, Judah received the land that included Gaza. Judah, however, couldn't take control of city because the Amalekites and Midianites were too strong (Joshua 15:47; Judges 1:18–19). Later, under Samuel's leadership, and even later during King Solomon's rule, God gave Israel control of much of the Philistine territory, including Gaza (1 Samuel 6:17; 1 Kings 4:24).

Throughout much of the Old Testament, the Assyrians, Egyptians, and Babylonians conquered and rebuilt Gaza repeatedly. Before Babylon attacked Judah and wiped out Gaza, fulfilling Jeremiah's warning, Pharoah Neco conquered Gaza in 609 BC. During intertestamental period, Gaza shifted hands between the Greeks, Syrians, and Egyptians. By Acts 8:26, the road from Jerusalem to Gaza was only a desert road. A new Gaza was built south of the old Gaza, but it was partially destroyed in AD 66. The new Gaza flourished in the second and third centuries but fell into Arab hands from AD 635 until the 1960s.[10] Even today, the "Gaza Strip" remains largely in contention with modern Israel.

Related passage: Acts 8:26

LAMENTATIONS

—❦—

2:6　Shelter from the Storm

In ancient times, a "garden booth" was a temporary shelter set up by farmers to protect their produce against harsh weather—rain, wind, or sun. Farmers drew upon basic designs and readily available materials such as sticks, shrubs, and branches to build their booths. This relatively simple construction lent booths an impermanent aspect. People could easily move or take down their booths once they had finished using them for the day. In Lamentations, when Jeremiah compared God's treatment of the tabernacle to a garden booth, the prophet meant to emphasize the disposable nature of the tabernacle in context of the people being exiled from the Promised Land (Lamentations 2:6).

The Bible makes clear that ancient people used booths in more than just a farming context. After Jacob reunited with Esau, he traveled to Succoth and prepared booths for his livestock (Genesis 33:17). Soldiers built booths as temporary abodes in the midst of their battles (1 Kings 20:12). And Uriah the Hittite reminded David that the ark of the covenant was in a booth (2 Samuel 11:11 ESV). Given the construction requirements for the tabernacle, however, we know that Israel housed the ark in a more substantial structure than a garden-variety booth. Uriah, like Jeremiah, was simply emphasizing the temporary nature of the ark's dwelling place at that time.

Related passages: Leviticus 23:34–44; Nehemiah 8:14–18

2:19   Dividing the Night

In the ancient Near East, an army approaching and attempting to scale the city wall overnight was a real threat, so the people sought ways to alert themselves to impending disaster. With no electricity, night vision, or alarm systems, major cities and military posts relied on the night watch for protection. The night watch generally began at sunset and lasted until sunrise, but no one person was expected to serve for the entire stretch. Instead, the night was divided into three or four segments (also called watches). Ancient Israel appears to have favored three segments, a conclusion based on the story of Gideon, who approached the Midianite army at the beginning of the middle watch. The first watch likely began at sunset, around 6 p.m.; the middle watch began around 10 p.m., while the final watch lasted from 2 a.m. to sunrise.

The Romans adopted a four-segmented night watch (Matthew 14:25), with each segment lasting only three hours instead of four. No doubt this offered the Romans more security, as each watchman had one less hour to stay awake in the night and, therefore, could be more alert during his assigned watch.

Related passages: Judges 7:19; Mark 6:48

4:2   Artistry in Everyday Life

Every established family in the ancient world possessed multiple pieces of pottery—bowls, jars, pots, baking disks, and pitchers. Such pieces were easy to form in a variety of sizes for use in the preparation and consumption of food and drink. Making pottery was a family affair early in human history, with the process involving simply shaping clay and putting it over fire to harden into a useable form. Clay was (and still is) easily available throughout much of the world, making pottery one of the cheapest and most common materials available. Therefore, ancient people didn't consider their earthenware pottery all that valuable; they could make replacement pieces without exerting too much energy.

Pottery is an ancient craft that became more sophisticated with the invention of the potter's wheel.

With the invention of the potter's wheel, making pottery developed into a professional trade. This new technology enabled potters to bring increased skill and detail to the formation of pieces, and it allowed pottery to be produced even more quickly than before. Potters used stones or broken pieces of pottery to shape each piece of clay in particular ways. And from very early, people made designs on their pottery—through carving or painting—in order to personalize and decorate it.

Related passages: Jeremiah 18:1–6; Romans 9:21; 2 Corinthians 4:7–9

4:10   Judgment Tastes of Death

When God entered into the Mosaic Covenant with His people, He gave them specifics about the blessings that would follow their obedience, as well as the curses that would come upon them should they disobey. One of those curses portrayed refined men and kind women resorting to cannibalizing their own children during a siege (Deuteronomy 28:53–57). As the southern kingdom of Judah sank further and further into rebellion, the prophets Jeremiah and Ezekiel repeatedly warned that cannibalism would come to God's people under judgment. And indeed, both

2 Kings 6:26–29 and Lamentations 4:10 portray this terrible practice occurring while Samaria and Jerusalem, the capital cities of the northern and southern kingdoms, were under siege from foreign armies.

Cannibalism, however, was never celebrated in the history of God's people. Furthermore, people throughout history have almost always associated cannibalism with evil, retribution, or judgment for wrongdoing. It should not surprise us that God's removal of His restraining hand in the face of repeated and egregious sin would end with sinful humans devouring one another. Interestingly, the Romans falsely accused Christians of cannibalism in the period of the early church because they spoke so often about eating the flesh and drinking the blood of Jesus (John 6:53–56)—merely a metaphor, of course, for the Lord's Supper.

Related passages: Jeremiah 19:9; Ezekiel 5:10

5:12 Humiliating Deaths

Lamentations records that Nebuchadnezzar's army brought complete destruction as they overran Jerusalem. Chapter 5 describes Jerusalem's leaders as being hung up by their hands in the wake of Nebuchadnezzar's assault. In this passage, one gets the picture of a rope draped over a gallows, a tree, or a wall with the corpse hanging from one end.

Hanging fallen leaders in some fashion was not uncommon in the ancient world. Joshua hung some of his enemies as he took over cities in the Promised Land (Joshua 8:29; 10:26). David followed the same practice centuries later (2 Samuel 4:12). In each of those cases, as in most similar ones, the hanging did not involve a live person but rather a corpse suspended in view of all the people to send a message to those still alive and to mark the price of rebellion. Not until the Greek and Roman periods does history record the hanging of live people for the purpose of a slow death, such as in the case of crucifixion.

Related passages: 2 Samuel 21:10–14; Esther 9:6–14

EZEKIEL

—❦—

4:12   Siege Bread Recipe

Bread, usually made of wheat or barley,[1] was a major staple in Israel. The people baked bread daily in pits with stones heated from cooking fires or in jar-like, clay hearths. God commissioned Ezekiel to visually communicate that He was going to cut off Jerusalem's food supply—"break the staff of bread" (Ezekiel 4:16). To illustrate this, Ezekiel first rationed grains and beans into meager measurements (4:9)—about eight ounces per day. Then he baked the rations over cow's dung—an upgrade from the human excrement God originally commanded.

Ancient Near Easterners commonly used animal dung for fuel when wood wasn't available. Once dry, dung mixed with straw burned slowly and naturally smelled unpleasant. However, cooking with animal dung did not stigmatize a person. On the other hand, "using human dung was considered repulsive."[2] Sadly, before Jerusalem was overtaken, its citizens became so badly besieged that wood became scarce, and dung was their only option for kindling. The use of dung in this way continues in the Middle East today.

Related passages: Leviticus 26:26; Lamentations 1:11

6:14   Where's Diblah?

The name Diblah is mentioned in the Bible only in Ezekiel 6:14, and scholars vary in their assessment of Diblah's location and description. Most contend Diblah doesn't actually exist. In Hebrew, the letters R and D are quite similar. Academics posit that due to scribal error, "Riblah"—a well-known location—was written incorrectly only in the book of Ezekiel.

If this assumption is correct, Ezekiel described a place rich with tragic history. In Riblah, pharaoh Neco imprisoned King Jehoahaz (2 Kings 23:33) and appointed a puppet king of Judah. Also in Riblah, Nebuchadnezzar captured Judah's king Zedekiah and put his sons to death before leading him away, blinded, to Babylon (25:6–7, 20–21). Geographically, Riblah is in the land of Hamath, located in what was formerly the northern border of Israel.

If indeed *Diblah* is correct—it is the name recorded in the ancient Masoretic Text—the land could have ties to a village in Galilee called Dibl.[3]

8:12   Carved Images

In the ancient Near East, carved images decorated pagan temples, shrines, and homes. Such carvings had no place in Yahweh's dwelling or among His people. In Leviticus 26:1, the Lord was clear: "You shall not make for yourselves idols, nor shall you set up for yourselves an image or a sacred pillar, nor shall you place a figured stone in your land to bow

Carved images, like this aegis of the Egyptian goddess, Neith, were often fashioned from precious metal or stone.

down to it; for I am the LORD your God." More than any other prophetic book, Ezekiel calls out idolatry as the nadir of unfaithfulness to God. Unfortunately, the prophet had many examples to indict. Ezekiel 8:12 describes Israelite elders systemically worshiping carved images in God's holy temple. Their hubris and audacity offended the Lord.

The word used for "carved images" is *maskith*, which means "image, idol, figure, picture, imagination, opinion, thoughts, conceit, imagery."[4] Thus, *maskith* means "carved image" in Ezekiel 8:12, "setting" in Proverbs 25:11, and "imagination" in Psalm 73:7. *Maskith's* field of meaning deftly accommodates both the physical reality of idols—the images were merely figures, devoid of life or animation—and the mental state of idolaters. Ascribing worship to a stone rather than the One who dwelt within the sanctuary required a vivid imagination.

Related passage: Proverbs 18:11

8:14 Who's Tammuz?

The women of Judah had no business weeping for the false god Tammuz anywhere, especially at the gate of the Lord's house. "Tammuz" is the Hebrew transliteration of the Sumerian word *Dumuzi*, the language of Tammuz's mythological origin. Biblically, the word occurs only in Ezekiel 8:14, though the fourth month of the Jewish calendar bore Tammuz's name as a result of Babylonian influence during the exile.

In ancient Near Eastern mythology, Tammuz, a shepherd, married the goddess Ishtar. When he died, Ishtar invaded the underworld to seek his release from Allatu, the Queen of Hades. According to the myth, growth ceased during Ishtar's underworld pursuit; therefore, Tammuz came to represent fertility and life. Annually, the king or governor sacredly married a chief priestess of Tammuz to ensure abundant crops and livestock. Also annually, women mourned Tammuz's "departure to the underworld" when the summer sun scorched the land.[5] The exact details surrounding Tammuz worship remain obscure, but by the time Judean women wept for Tammuz at the temple gate, the cult was centuries old.

10:10   Cherubim

Cherubim, the plural word for *cherub*, appears in the Bible fifty-eight times. The majority of mentions occur in the book of Ezekiel; only one occurs in the New Testament (Hebrews 9:5). Scholars are unsettled as to the precise definition, but most surmise it may mean "intercessor" or "to praise."[6] Cherubim make their first appearance early in the biblical narrative as gatekeepers of Eden after Adam and Eve's banishment (Genesis 3:24). Cherubim images adorned holy adornments in Moses' tabernacle and Solomon's temple: carvings of cherubim covered its doors, walls, and stands, and two cherubim are carved into the ark of the covenant (Exodus 25:22; 26:1, 31). The Psalms describe the Lord as enthroned above the cherubim, riding on the wings of the wind (Psalm 18:10). In general, cherubim appear to guard that which is holy.

Ezekiel described the cherubim as bearing the throne of God with several sets of wings and either two (Ezekiel 41:18) or four (10:14) faces: a man and a lion and additionally an ox and an eagle. Some scholars compare cherubim's description with the hybrid man/beast figures in Assyrian, Egyptian, and Babylonian cultures,[7] but the cherubim remain unique in their composition and function.

Related passages: 2 Chronicles 3:7, 10 – 13; Psalm 80:1; 99:1

13:18   Magic Bands and Veils of Divination

The Hebrew terms for "magic bands" (*keseth*) and "veils of divination" (*mispachah*) are examples of *hapax legomena* — words that occur in only one passage in Scripture. Scholars universally hold that both veils of divination and magic bands were amulets, or charms, of idolatry, but scholars differ on precisely what type. In general, the amulets were "intended to bring about untimely deaths, expressed as 'hunting for souls [i.e., lives].'"[8] The Lord detested magic bands and veils of divination, not only because their use was a direct affront to His sovereignty, but also because those who made and sold these trinkets misled and preyed on the innocent (Ezekiel 13:19 – 20). The bands and veils diametrically opposed God's Law in both symbolism and use.

The false prophetesses' bands and veils bear an interesting comparison to the description of God's commands in Deuteronomy 6:8: "You shall bind [God's commands] as a sign on your hand and they shall be as frontals on your forehead." To this day, during weekday prayers, Jewish men put on *tefellin* or phylacteries—small boxes worn on the forehead or arm that contain portions of Hebrew scripture.[9] This practice is intended to honor God's Law and to remember His deliverance of Israel from Egypt.

Related passages: Deuteronomy 18:10; Jeremiah 29:8–9

18:2   Sour Grapes

In Ezekiel 18:2, the prophet referenced a colloquial expression about sour grapes common to his original audience. The word *qahah*—"blunt"—speaks to the negative blunting, numbing effect of the fathers' consumption of sour grapes.[10] This adage, also used in Jeremiah 31:29–30, expresses the notion that subsequent generations bear the repercussions of their forbears' sins. This theological conclusion probably finds its roots in Exodus 20:5 and Deuteronomy 5:9.

Young grapes are often sour.

However, in the context of both Jeremiah and Ezekiel, God directly refuted the idea that "the children's teeth are set on edge" *because* of their fathers; instead, God exhorted that each individual is responsible for his or her own actions. This may seem at odds with the Exodus and Deuteronomy passages, until one reads the corresponding blessing that follows the discipline in each: God shows "lovingkindness to thousands, to those who love Me and keep My commandments" (Exodus 20:6; Deuteronomy 5:10). In harmony with the Law (Deuteronomy 24:16), Ezekiel refuted an old adage in order to indict his audience for being numb to idolatry and chide them to take responsibility for following God rather than settling for a legacy of sour grapes.[11]

Related passages: Exodus 34:7; Ezekiel 18:14–18

20:29   What's *Bamah*?

Hebrew for "high place," *bamah* indicated elevated areas in the ancient Near East that were used for ritual cultic worship. Nefarious kings and commoners practiced idolatry openly by erecting high places despite living in the Promised Land. Righteous monarchs, on the other hand, proved their devotion by tearing down these idol shrines.

Although the Old Testament often references "high places," Ezekiel 20:29 is the only passage where *bamah* is transliterated and utilized as a formal place name. In this passage, Ezekiel used the term to continue his message of God's indictment of Israelite idolatry and employ alliteration that is lost in English but would have readily been recognized in Hebrew: *Mah* **habamah** *asher atem* **habaim**. This phrase is literally translated, "What is this high place you go to?"[12] The repetition of sounds in Hebrew highlights the continuous action of pursuing idolatry.

Related passages: 1 Kings 11:7; 12:31; 2 Kings 17:9; 18:4; 23:5–8

28:1–19   Tyre: Person, Place, or Thing?

Ezekiel 28 is one of the most difficult passages to interpret. Scholars have long debated exactly who God was addressing in this oracle and lament.

Craggy coastline of Tyre

Most point to either a specific person, a demon, Satan, or a representative of the entire country.

- *A Specific Person.* Ezekiel could have been referring specifically to the Phoenician ruler Ethbaal III, who reigned over Tyre during the time of Ezekiel's prophesying.

- *A Demon.* Because the first half of Ezekiel's address refers to Tyre's prince and references Eden, some think this passage addresses a demon. This interpretation looks to the book of Daniel, which refers to angels and demons as "princes" (Daniel 10:13; 21:1).

- *Satan.* The same argument for Tyre being a demon applies here, with the further notion that the prince and king both allude to Satan. As a fallen angel, Satan could ostensibly have been present with God in Eden.

- *A Representative.* Finally, some believe Ezekiel was addressing Tyre's leadership as a way to address the whole country. Surrounded by water, the country had a natural fortress against enemies, as well as opportunities for seafaring commerce and a thriving fishing economy. Therefore, Tyre took pride in its navy, wealth, and seeming impenetrability. The simplest explanation is often the most elegant and precise. The text addresses the prince/king of Tyre; therefore, this interpretation is the most likely.

40–43   Ezekiel's Temple: Past or Future?

The Lord provided an angelic guide to take Ezekiel through a new temple in the future. In chapters 40–43, Ezekiel recorded the composition, dimensions, and specific purposes for each part of the temple and its grounds. His prophecy culminated with the return of the Lord's presence. Many ask: Has this temple already been built, or is it yet to be constructed?

After the exile, some Jews returned to rebuild the temple (Ezra 1; 3:2–11). Although blessed by God, this second temple failed to restore the temple to its former glory (3:12). In 19 BC, Herod the Great began a complete remodel of the second temple to curry favor with the Jews. In AD 70, however, Rome destroyed the temple. The temple hasn't been rebuilt since. The second temple was never characterized as being inhabited by God. As a result, many pre-millennial scholars believe—and their view is most feasible—Ezekiel described a physical temple that will be built in the future, during the millennial reign of Christ. At that time, Jerusalem—the city where the temple will be located—will be restored as the place where God dwells. Once again, the nations will look to Jerusalem to know the Lord.[13]

Related passages: Zechariah 8:1–8, 20–23

Ezekiel 40:38–43; 45:18–25   Sacrifices in the Temple: Why?

When Ezekiel toured the future temple, he surveyed an area for sacrificing animals. Since the temple in his vision has yet to be built, but Jesus' incarnation, crucifixion, and resurrection have already occurred, the idea that sacrifices will be necessary is perplexing.

Hebrews 10:4 states that "it is impossible for the blood of bulls and goats to take away sins." Therefore, animal sacrifice, even before Christ, was *never* sufficient to atone for sin. Further, early believers, including

In the Old Testament, sheep were often sacrificed in anticipation of Christ's death. In the kingdom, animal sacrifices will serve as a memorial.

the apostle Paul, participated in temple sacrifices (Acts 21:26). Animal sacrifice merely served as a temporary system in which atonement was given on credit until Jesus died to pay the bill. (Romans 3:23–26).

The temple in Ezekiel's vision and the resumption of sacrifices in the thousand-year reign of Christ will be powerful components of God's plan for the righteous Jewish remnant—to reinstitute His presence in the temple as part of of His restoration of Israel. Temple sacrifices will reinforce the symbolic holiness of God and mankind's need for atonement through Christ.

Today, Christians commemorate Jesus' death through communion, and in this way, proclaim His death until He returns. Similarly, the reinstitution of temple sacrifices and feast days in the millennium will serve as a distinctly Jewish memorial to Jesus' sacrificial atonement for sin. These sacrifices will begin after Israel is restored and regains "prominence in God's plan" (Romans 11:25–27), and "will appropriately reflect Israelite worship (Ezekiel 45:18–25), though there will not be a reinstitution of the Old Covenant (Romans 10:4)." [14]

Related passages: Exodus 12:1–14; Leviticus 23:5–8, 39–43; Numbers 28:16–25; 29:12–38

DANIEL

———— ✿ ————

1:4 Private Education

Nebuchadnezzar's training academy plunged Daniel and his fellow selected Israelites deep into the literature and language of the Chaldeans. Their Babylonian education lasted three years and prepared them to serve in the king's court but differed significantly from the education they would have received at home or elsewhere in the ancient Near East.

Archaeologists have found educational texts dating back to 2500 BC, which provide evidence of schools for scribes in ancient Sumer and Egypt. Such schools were often attached to the pagan temples at which they worshiped their "gods" and divided into elementary education—where children learned writing, literature, and how to copy—and higher education—where youths studied composition, geography, and science.

Ancient Israelites initially reserved formal education for priests. Such training was often carried out at the temple of God. Samuel, for instance, began his education as an apprentice to Eli the priest at the temple (1 Samuel 1:28; 3:1). Priests needed to be well trained because they were responsible for transmitting the Law and training God's people to understand it. About the time of the exile (when Ezra served as a priest *and* as a scribe), scribes became the primary people responsible for passing down God's Law in written and oral form. Therefore, a formal division of scribes began to emerge. Israelites admired scribes because they accurately copied and taught God's words (Ezra 7:6–11).

A Bar Mitzvah ceremony, signaling membership in the Jewish community following a period of Hebrew and Torah study

In Israel, those who did not enter formal training to become priests or scribes primarily looked to their homes for education. The goal of education for this group was to know and worship God. The content was the Torah, and the teachers were parents who passed on God's revelation. Prophets, with Moses as a model, were also considered teachers, because they proclaimed and applied revelation from God. Though education in Israel didn't cover the sciences, many young people learned trades like metallurgy, mining, building, and wood and stonework (Exodus 35:30–35). Formal schools, enrolling kids as young as six or seven, didn't develop in Israel until the intertestamental period, around the third century BC.[1]

Related passages: Deuteronomy 6:7; Proverbs 1:7; Zechariah 7:12

1:7 A New Name

In the Old Testament, name changes signified a change in allegiance, a new relationship or phase in life, or a new role or vocation. Abram, "exalted father," became Abraham, "exalted father of a multitude," signifying his role as the recipient of God's covenant promise and as the father of the nation of Israel. Jacob, "the crafty one" who cheated his brother out of the birthright and inheritance, became Israel, meaning "God fights," because he wrestled with God and won (Genesis 32:27). In these and other Old Testament instances, the one performing the name change is usually God or an authoritative figure, as in the case of Daniel and his friends.

Nebuchadnezzar tried to change Daniel's and his friends' identities and allegiance to the Lord by moving them to a new land and giving them new names. Daniel, which means "my God is judge," became Belteshazzar, which probably means "Bel's Prince." Daniel's three friends, whose names all made reference to Yahweh, received names connected to Babylonian idols. Ultimately, however, Nebuchadnezzar's scheme failed.

In the New Testament, a significant name change followed the conversion of Saul, the persecutor of Christ followers. In that case Jesus changed Saul's name, which means "the asked for one," to Paul, which means "small." This change signified the humbling that took place in Paul's heart when Jesus appeared to him on the way to Damascus, and Paul's calling to suffer for Christ as the apostle to the Gentiles (Romans 11:13).

In the future, Jerusalem and all believers will receive new names from God, signifying our new characters and our new, perfect allegiance to the Lord.[2]

Related passages: Genesis 17:5; Isaiah 62:2; 65:15; Revelation 2:17

1:8   The King's Banquet

In Babylon, Daniel and his friends could have eaten like kings. But for good reasons, they refused to eat from King Nebuchadnezzar's banquet. First, since the Babylonian king was a pagan, his wine and meat had likely been dedicated to pagan idols before making its way to the dinner table. God prohibited the worship of idols (Exodus 20:4–6), so when pagans dedicated food to idols as a part of worship, the act defiled the food. As devout worshipers of the Lord, Daniel and his friends didn't want to take part in any pagan rituals; they wanted to please God. Second, the king's banquet most likely included ceremonially unclean food, such as camels, rabbits, pigs, marine animals without both fins and scales, dead animals, and others, according to Mosaic Law. The fact that Daniel and his friends risked their lives to remain ceremonially pure proved that they were faithful followers of the Lord. God honored and gave favor to Daniel and his friends for obeying Him (Daniel 1:20).[3]

In the New Testament, Jesus fulfilled the Mosaic Law and declared all food clean (Acts 10:11–15). As a result, Paul instructed Christians to follow their consciences when deciding whether or not to eat food sacrificed to idols, always keeping in mind believers with weak faith so as not to cause them to question their faith (1 Corinthians 8:4–13).

Related passage: Leviticus 11:1–47

2:1   The King's Dream

In the Old Testament, dreams were believed to often be a conduit of divine revelation. God gave a warning to Abimelech in a dream (Genesis 20:3, 6). In Jacob's dream, the Lord revealed the stairway connecting heaven and earth (28:12). God communicated important information about the future to Joseph through a dream (37:5–11; 40:7–19).

When God gave King Nebuchadnezzar a dream or a series of dreams about a giant statue, the earthly king trembled at its possible significance. In the ancient Near East, good dreams signified divine favor and bad dreams, divine displeasure.[4] Clueless as to the meaning of his dreams, King Nebuchadnezzar feared a bad interpretation and the gods' displeasure. The king called his astrologers to interpret the dream. Ancient astrologers made predictions about the future based on the courses of the sun, moon, stars, and planets. After these astrologers failed, Daniel helped Nebuchadnezzar understand his dream as a template for prophecy and future world history; Daniel also made it clear that the king's dreams and their interpretations came from the one, true God (Daniel 2:28).

Related passage: Numbers 12:6

2:4   The Official Language of Babylon

From Daniel 2:4 to 7:28, Daniel switched from writing in Hebrew to writing in Aramaic, the primary language used in business and government throughout the Babylonian Empire. Because Daniel was a high government official, he probably spoke and wrote in Aramaic in his official capacity.

Archaeologists have discovered Aramaic inscriptions dating to 850 BC in Syria. And by the time of the Persian Empire, Aramaic had become the empire's official language.[5] Nonetheless, Daniel's use of Aramaic in a large portion of his book seems surprising, given he had a Hebrew audience. When God's people were taken captive by the Babylonians, they lived in some sense of subjection to the next three world empires: Medo-Persian, Greek, and Roman. In Daniel 2:4–7:28,

Latin, Greek, and Aramaic inscriptions on stone in Palmyra, Syria

Daniel recorded the prophetic future of the world—a time during which these Gentile empires would, in essence, rule the world—and rule Israel. It makes sense, therefore, that because Daniel was writing about the future world ruled by Gentiles, he used words that would be understandable to Gentiles. On the other hand, Daniel wrote chapters 1 and 8–12 in Hebrew because this important information was meant specifically for God's people.

In addition to Daniel, part of Ezra was written in Aramaic. These chapters record mostly correspondence with Persian officials, whom Ezra wrote to in Aramaic. And after their long exile, God's people had become accustomed to using Aramaic instead of Hebrew.

Related passage: Ezra 4–7

3:24   The Fiery Furnace

The fiery furnace in Daniel chapter 3 was most likely used for smelting metals. However, according to Jeremiah 29:22, these types of furnaces were also used for capital punishment. Nebuchadnezzar's evil use of his, therefore, wouldn't have necessarily been surprising. Nebuchadnezzar's furnace had an opening at the top, into which metal materials were thrown, and an opening at the bottom to take out the cast metal. King Nebuchadnezzar could see Shadrach, Meshach, and Abed-nego plus their angelic protector through one of the furnace's two openings. Other types of furnaces and ovens in Old Testament times were used to bake bricks and pottery or cook meals.[6]

Related passages: Genesis 15:17; 19:28

6:16   Lion Down on the Job

In Daniel's day, a lions' den like the one King Darius was forced to throw his trusted prime minister into, was a pit in which lions were kept. Assyrian and Babylonian kings kept lions as pets, for hunting, or for punishing criminals. The Medo-Persian kings continued to use lions as

An image of a lion near the Babylonian Ishtar Gate

a means of capital punishment.[7] After throwing criminals into the den, officials covered the opening of the den with a stone (Daniel 6:17).

Lions were a fairly familiar sight in the ancient Near East and were feared because of their strength and speed (6:27). The Bible records several incidents of lions attacking people, though lion attacks were rare. In fact, lions were more likely to attack helpless sheep than human beings. In 1 Kings 13:23–25, a disobedient prophet was killed by a lion as God's punishment. In 1 Kings 20:35–36, a man refused to obey a prophet's command and was killed by a lion. In 2 Kings 17:25–26, the foreigners who had settled in Samaria after God's people were deported to Assyria refused to worship God, so he sent lions to kill some of them.

Related passage: Genesis 49:9; 1 Samuel 17:34–37

7:2   Four Winds

As Daniel dreamed, God gave him a vision of a great windstorm stirring above the Mediterranean Sea (the "great sea"). Daniel's original audience would have recognized the "four winds of heaven" as four literal winds coming from different parts of the ancient world. First, the *north* wind was the coldest wind that brought in the rain (Proverbs 25:23) and blew mostly in October. This rain watered the land and helped crops to flourish. Second, the *east* wind was the hot wind that blew from across the sweltering Arabian Desert. Third, the *south* wind was also a hot wind that blew from the southeast and southwest and signaled a hot, spring day. Fourth, the *west* wind brought moisture from the Mediterranean Sea.[8]

In the ancient Near East, the sea represented the chaotic, human world of conflict, unrest, and evil. The four winds in Daniel's vision represented God's sovereign control, not only over the weather and the natural world but over all of human history, including the future kingdoms which would come to power, represented by the four beasts in Daniel's vision.

In the New Testament, when the Lord's disciples faced deadly storm winds, Jesus calmed the winds with a word, demonstrating His deity and power over nature (Luke 8:23–25).

Related passage: Daniel 7:3

7:9–10   A Vision of God's Throne

Daniel's vision in chapter 7 featured God the Father, the Ancient of Days, taking His seat on His heavenly throne. God's throne burned with fire signifying His holiness. A river of fire flowed from it, showing the righteous judgment that issued from His judgment seat (Daniel 7:10). The flaming wheels on the heavenly throne illustrated God's omnipresence and unlimited power (7:9).

Daniel wasn't the only one to see God's throne. As Isaiah sought the Lord in the temple, he had a vision of God sitting on his heavenly throne. In Revelation 4:1–6, John peered into God's throne room and saw His throne surrounded by fire, lightning, and thunder, and encircled by supernatural beings eternally occupied by worship.

Earthly thrones in Daniel's day may have lacked the river of fire and the flaming wheels of God's throne, but they were glorious in their own right. In a culture where most ordinary people sat or reclined on cushions on the ground, judges, military chiefs, and kings sat on thrones, indicating their authority (Genesis 41:40). Royal thrones were the most magnificent. They were elevated, displayed detailed workmanship, used expensive materials, and often had a rounded top. Kings sat on their thrones, dressed in royal robes, to carry out their official duties (Acts 12:21).[9]

Related passages: 1 Kings 10:19; Isaiah 6:1

11:1–45   Kings of the North and Kings of the South

Daniel's vision in chapter 11, which was much more detailed than his previous ones, revealed that before the kings of the north and south began fighting, a "mighty king" would arise and overthrow the Medo-Persian Empire (Daniel 11:1–3), as well as Asia Minor, Syria, and Egypt. From history we know that the "mighty king" was Alexander the Great, the powerful ruler of Macedonia. After Alexander the Great died, his four

First century BC mosaic representing the battle of Alexander the Great against Darius (III) the Great, found in Pompeii in the House of the Faun, now in the Museo Archeologico Nazionale (Naples)

military generals, Seleucus, Ptolemy, Lysimachus, and Cassander, divided his kingdom. Two of these four generals became more powerful than the others. Seleucus headed the Seleucid dynasty, which ruled over Syria and Mesopotamia, and Ptolemy headed the Ptolemaic dynasty which ruled from Egypt. Daniel 11 details the ongoing battles between the "kings of the south," or the Ptolemaic Dynasty, and the "kings of the north," or the Seleucid dynasty. The Ptolemies ruled from 323–145 BC, and the Seleucids reigned from 312–163 BC. For almost 300 years, God's people got caught in the crosshairs of these two battling dynasties.[10]

Related passages: Daniel 7:13–14; 10:1–21; 12:1–2

HOSEA

—❈—

1:2–3   His Wife Was a What?

The book of Hosea begins with a shocking command—Hosea was to marry "a wife of harlotry" who would give birth to children of harlotry.

The ancient Near East didn't offer many options for women to earn a living, which left widows and foreign women vulnerable to prostitution. Sadly, ritualistic prostitution was also common. Heathens perverted sex acts into worship to Baal. Even God's chosen people indulged themselves; for example, Tamar posed as a temple prostitute to gain justice—and an heir—from Judah (Genesis 38:12–21).

Zenunim is the Hebrew word translated "harlotry" (and "prostitution"). The term is plural, which adds intensity and indicates a repeated pattern—not just a single act but a lifestyle of immorality. Scripture applies the term to Gomer because of her perpetual two-timing. It is also used elsewhere to refer to Assyria's luring other nations into spiritual infidelity (Nahum 3:4). Exactly what kind of harlot Gomer was is difficult to ascertain. Some theorize she may have been a temple prostitute prior to marriage. Others suggest she was a perpetual adulterer or a pagan worshiper.[1]

Related passages: Jeremiah 3:8–9

This stollen is the German version of fruitcake. There's more flour and less grain than *ashishot.*

3:1   Ancient Fruitcake

In ancient Israel, there was no better way to encourage obedience to God's command to be fruitful and multiply than by handing a raisin cake to a happy couple. This cake, prepared with grains, dried fruits, and spices, was considered a delicacy and, more interestingly, an aphrodisiac. Song of Solomon 2:5 notes that raisin cakes could revive the love-sick. King David distributed raisin cakes to the Israelites after he retrieved the ark of the covenant—a time of fervent celebration and praise (1 Chronicles 16:3).

Pagans incorporated raisin cakes, or *ashishot* in Hebrew, into their worship. "Raisin cakes were used as cultic offerings by many ancient Near Easterners, and were especially prominent in ancient Near Eastern fertility rites."[2] Thus, the Lord's words to Hosea that the sons of Israel had turned to other gods and loved raisin cakes held a double allusion: the Israelites had practiced cultic worship instead of fidelity to God, and they had pursued and prized sensuality.

Related passage: 2 Samuel 6:19

7:11   Silly Doves

Hosea used the phrase "silly doves" to highlight the flightiness of a people so disconnected from God and so ruled by fear that they flew to their enemies, Egypt and Assyria, to beg for protection. Doves commonly symbolized naïveté, and Israel's trust in nations who hated them proved they were supremely dove-like.

The Bible first mentions doves as post-flood scouts in Genesis 8 — Noah knew the waters had fully receded when the dove didn't return. For the poor, doves served as acceptable substitutes for more expensive animals used in worship in the temple (Leviticus 5:7; 12:8).

Doves also served multiple metaphorical purposes in the Bible. Song of Solomon uses "dove" as a term of endearment and beauty, while Psalms uses a dove's wings to represent freedom and beauty. In Isaiah and Nahum, the moans of doves represent the distress of the people. In Matthew, Jesus warned His disciples to "be shrewd as serpents and innocent as doves" (Matthew 10:16) and the Holy Spirit descended on Jesus "as a dove" (3:16). This connotation of innocence persists to this day.

Related passages: Genesis 8:8–12; Hosea 11:11

8:6   Divine Calves

Through Hosea, God reminded Israel that they deserved recompense for their past blatant idolatry when they worshiped the "calf of Samaria." At that point in history, the nation of Israel had split into two kingdoms, partly because Jeroboam — who took control of the northern kingdom, Israel — seized the opportunity for a coup d'état. Fearing the people would return to the southern kingdom, Judah, to worship God in Jerusalem, Jeroboam erected two golden calves — one in Dan and one in Bethel — and presented the idols as gods (1 Kings 12:28–30). In Hosea 8:6, "Samaria" represents the northern kingdom.

Not coincidentally, the Assyrians, who eventually conquered the northern kingdom, took the golden calf at Bethel as a souvenir (Hosea 10:6). Because the people of Israel put their faith in a human-made idol, foreign idolaters would sweep the land of false gods. Yahweh was so disgusted with His people's worship of the golden calf at Bethel — translated "house of God" — that He referred to the location as "Beth-aven," which means "house of evil."

Related passages: Exodus 32:24; 2 Kings 10:29; 2 Chronicles 13:8

9:4 Tainted Bread, Tainted Worship

Numbers 19:11–22 describes in detail the process of purification or isolation for those who came in contact with dead bodies. God's stringent laws concerning contact with the dead served a dual purpose: first, the laws inferred God's absolute holiness — His people reflected His holiness by separating and cleansing themselves from death, the result of sin. Secondly, the laws created a hygienic and emotional buffer for mourners, since in ancient Israel, relatives prepared the deceased for burial.

The tainted nature of mourners' bread is mentioned in the context of the Law, uncleanness, and unacceptable offerings. Hosea prophesied that the people of Israel were destined for grief due to their unfaithfulness to God; therefore, their offerings would persistently be as unclean as bread in the household of a dead body. The double isolation of a sin-stained, idolatrous people, languishing in exile far from the temple of God, rendered any feigned attempt at worship as unfit for God's consumption — their offerings would only satisfy themselves.

JOEL

―❈―

1:4 The Appetite of Locusts

Similar in appearance and, usually, in behavior to grasshoppers, locusts have long plagued civilizations, particularly in the desert areas of Africa, the Middle East, and Asia. Although locusts are normally solitary creatures, when environmental conditions align, they enter a "gregarious" phase, meaning they become simultaneously hyper-social and hungry. Gregarious locusts migrate in thick groups numbering tens of *millions* and fly hundreds of miles daily, consuming everything in their path and leaving economic and agricultural devastation in their wake.[1] In 1875, the largest, most devastating swarm recorded decimated parts of Missouri, Kansas, Colorado, and Nebraska. The swarm was "1,800 miles long and 110 miles wide, equaling the combined area of Connecticut, Delaware, Maine, Maryland, Massachusetts, New Hampshire, New Jersey, New York, Pennsylvania, Rhode Island and Vermont."[2]

Locusts make several appearances in Scripture. In Deuteronomy, when God declared to Israel that they would be cursed with locusts should they stray from Him, they were already well acquainted with the way the creatures devoured land (Deuteronomy 28:38). They had witnessed locusts' insatiable ravaging when Yahweh plagued Egypt before the exodus (Exodus 10:12–15). Joel also wrote about locusts, although readers who examine multiple translations will notice right away that the word the prophet used for "locusts"—*arbeh* in Hebrew—eludes precise definition.[3] Some scholars assert that the different locust labels denote a progression of locust life, from the all-ravaging mature locusts to the their tiny offspring (see NIV, KJV). Others surmise that the labels describe the specific methods of devastation that locusts use—gnawing, swarming, creeping, and stripping (see NASB, NLT). Every translation, however, agrees on the locusts' effect: total devastation.

Related passages: 1 Kings 8:37; Psalm 105:33–35; Nahum 3:15–17

1:14   Solemn Assembly

The Hebrew word for "solemn assembly" is *atzarah*, from the root—*atzar*—which means "to restrain."[4] Thus, a solemn assembly's emphasis was rooted in restraint. Such groups united themselves in fasting from food, work, or sex and in reflecting upon Scripture and confessing their sins to God. Solemn assemblies were incorporated into the holy days like the eighth day of the Feast of Booths (Leviticus 23:36; Numbers 29:35; Deuteronomy 31:10–13) and the seventh day of Passover (Deuteronomy 16:8). However, solemn assemblies were not limited to holy days. Israelite leaders proclaimed solemn assemblies any time the people needed reminders of God's Law or His deeds in order to be compelled to repent (1 Samuel 7:6; Jeremiah 36:9). Unfortunately, solemn assemblies could also be used negatively. Jehu, king of Israel, declared an idolatrous one to worship Baal (2 Kings 10:20).

Joel had to instruct the people to prepare a solemn assembly because they had strayed so far from God's Law that they had forgotten how to fast and pray and how to recognize God's discipline. Had they regularly read God's Law, they would have known that the desolation of the land by locust swarms was a result of their unfaithfulness—they were under God's curse (Deuteronomy 28:15–19).

Related passages: 2 Chronicles 7:9; Nehemiah 8:18; Joel 2:15

3:8 Who Were the Sabeans?

The name "Sabean" appears only three times in the Bible. Two of those occur in the context of prophecy, which gives some weight to the mysterious people group. Scholars differ concerning the Sabeans' background. Some say Sabeans were of North African origin, while others hypothesize that they were from southern Arabia.[5] Scholars are in agreement, however, that the Sabeans were known for the trade of goods like precious gems, gold, and spices. The Sabeans are also known as the people of Sheba (1 Kings 10:1–13) or Seba (1 Chronicles 1:9). Their first mention by this name takes place in Genesis 10, where Seba is listed as one of the descendants of Cush, from Ham's line, and Sheba is listed as one of the descendants of Joktan, from Shem's line. Psalm 72:10 mentions both the kings of Sheba and Seba giving gifts to Solomon, representing nations at "the ends of the earth" (Psalm 72:8). Their mention together may infer their kinship to one another or their geographical proximity. In either case,

The Sabeans were merchants of spices.

Joel 3:8 indicates that Tyre and Sidon and all the regions of Philistia would be repaid for enslaving Israelites by being enslaved to the far-away Sabeans.

Related passages: Genesis 10:28; Job 1:15; Isaiah 43:3; 45:14

AMOS

------ ✦ ------

1:2   So What If Mount Carmel Dries Up?

Like the Statue of Liberty, the Eiffel Tower, or the White House today, in the world of the Old Testament, Mount Carmel was a significant symbol and landmark, recognized far and wide. When ancient Near Eastern travelers spied its peaks, they knew they were in the northern kingdom of Israel—the place where Saul made a monument for himself (1 Samuel 15:12); where David met his wife, Abigail (25:2–42); and where Elijah challenged the priests of Baal (1 Kings 18:17–40). The mount not only held great significance in the nation's history; it also represented beauty and prosperity. King Solomon testified to the beauty of its rolling hills and water-fed, robust foliage when he wrote of his love, "Your head crowns you like Carmel" (Song of Solomon 7:5).

Amos' prophecy that Mount Carmel would dry up had to be met with disbelief. Mount Carmel running dry would be as shocking to the ancient Israelites as Niagara Falls turning to dust. The area's greenness was such a dependable sight. However, God's promises are infinitely more dependable, and Mount Carmel will indeed dry up as a part of His judgment for Israel's faithlessness (Deuteronomy 28:24).

Related passage: Nahum 1:4

1:3   Oracles Come in Threes . . . and Fours

"For three transgressions . . . and for four" appears eight times in the book of Amos. Although this kind of construction is employed in other biblical genres, such as in the poetry of the psalms (Psalm 62:11–12) and the wisdom of the proverbs (Proverbs 6:16; 30:15–16, 18–19, 21–23, 29–31), it is virtually exclusive to Amos within the prophetic genre. Only Micah 5:5–6 also includes this pattern, which usually represents fullness. Rather than using the pattern to list several specific features, biblical writers most often used it to emphasize the *last* feature—and thereby the extremity—of a particular subject.[1] The pattern can enumerate the overflow of something good, like the majesty of wild animals (Proverbs 30:29–31), or something negative, like unquenchable greed (30:15–16).

Amos reserved the most ominous use of this number pattern for his *oracles*—messages of judgment. The prophet used the pattern to emphasize the fullness of the abominations of the Gentile nations and Judah. By only naming their last abomination, the prophet highlighted each nation's last-straw offense. Then, like a camera panning over a wide scene, then zooming in until it focuses on a single subject, God, through Amos, fixed His harshest gaze upon the northern kingdom of Israel. Only Israel's oracle specifically enumerates all *seven* abominations (Amos 2:6–8, 12). That Israel was the last in Amos' oracles, that their transgressions outweighed the gentiles, and that the prophet fully listed their sins, served as the ultimate warning that Israel's sin had undeniably garnered the wrath of God.

Related passage: Job 5:19

4:1 Cows of Bashan: Who Were These Heifers?

Bashan, which means "fertile plain,"[2] was a lovely, verdant stretch of land originally given to the half-tribe of Manasseh (Joshua 13:29–31). Situated between the borders of Gilead and Mount Hermon, Bashan was known for its towering oaks and lush greenery. The cattle that grazed there were, by virtue of the bountiful land they fed upon, stronger and fatter than average, much like grass-fed cows today. This fact led the psalmist to describe the bulls of Bashan as possessing the ferocity of lions (Psalm 22:12–13).

Although grass-fed beef is desirable in many modern cultures, when Amos addressed the women of the northern kingdom of Israel as "cows of Bashan," he did not intend it as a compliment. Rather, the prophet was specifically addressing their exploitative greed—they were world-renowned for growing fat by victimizing the poor and needy.

Related passage: Ezekiel 39:18

5:8   Pleiades and Orion

For the original recipients of Amos' dirge, the constellation Orion and Pleiades, the bright cluster of stars in Taurus, kept time and portended the seasons like a faithful watch and calendar. "The rising of Pleiades before daybreak signaled the return of spring while the rising of Orion after sunset heralded the onset of winter." [3] Amos described the Pleiades and Orion as part of the created order—proof of God's faithfulness and under His command. However, many in the ancient Near East, viewed the stars themselves as deities.

The constellation of Pleiades

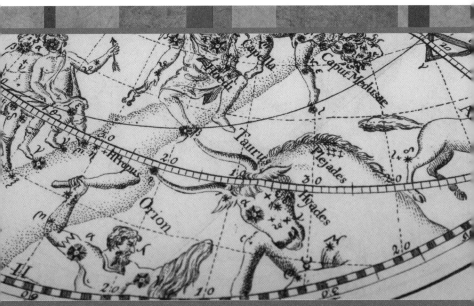

The mention of the Pleiades and Orion in Amos 5:8 also serves a metonymical purpose. With just this reference, Amos challenged his listeners to remember the beginning—the creation account in Genesis 1. Amos' point was clear: the One who created light itself (Genesis 1:3–5) was also all-powerful to bring about His judgement.

Related passage: Isaiah 44:24

5:26 Sikkuth and Kiyyun—Who Were They?

Amos filled chapter 5 of his prophecy with references to the natural world—fire, wormwood, stars, water—and he included in each reference one uniting truth: everything in nature exists in subjection to its Creator. At the end of chapter 5, Amos referenced two more natural elements under the Lord's subjection, two celestial bodies named Sikkuth and Kiyyun. These entities are associated with the planet Saturn and its surrounding stars. People groups in the ancient Near East, specifically in Assyria, regarded Sikkuth and Kiyyun as gods and worshiped them. [4] The precise meaning of the names of these two false gods is unknown, but according to some scholars, the words *Sikkuth* and *Kiyyun* had an interchangeable quality, denoting either an inanimate object or a deity. These scholars note, "The words 'shrine' and 'pedestal' could be translated as 'Sakkuth' and 'Kaiwan,'" [5] alternate spellings for *Sikkuth* and *Kiyyun*.

In other words, Amos 5:26 could be translated, and has been in the New International Version, "You have lifted up the shrine of your king, the pedestal of your idols, the star of your god—which you made for yourselves."

Related passages: Exodus 20:3; Judges 10:13; Jeremiah 25:6; Daniel 11:37

OBADIAH

Obadiah 3   In the Cleft of the Rock

Edom (now part of modern Jordan) sits immediately to the east of southern Israel. A ridge of mountains runs north and south through that area, from just south of the Dead Sea to the Gulf of Aqaba. These mountains form the primary inhabitable area of Edom, as the majority of the rain falls on the western edge of these peaks. Ancient Edomites likewise lived along the mountain ridge, where the potential for growing crops was best. And they often made their homes in clefts or caves in the mountainsides.

"The Monastery" in Petra, Jordan, stands in ancient Edom.

While cave dwelling may not sound appealing to modern ears, caves promised an extra measure of security for ancient people, particularly in the face of invading armies. Living in a cave on a mountainside allowed people to hide easily. And if cave dwellers were seen, their abodes provided a strong position from which to defend themselves. These circumstances led biblical writers to use the image of these lofty dwellings repeatedly throughout Scripture, both literally and metaphorically. The Lord spoke to the cave-dwelling Edomites through Obadiah, condemning their arrogance and confidence in their own power and the strength of their earthly defenses. In Jeremiah, the Lord proclaimed that He would bring down those who hid in the clefts with deceiving arrogance in their hearts (Jeremiah 49:16). In Exodus, the Lord put Moses in the cleft of the rock and covered it with His hand to protect the leader from seeing the full glory of the Lord's face (Exodus 33:20–23).

Related passages: 1 Samuel 22:1; 1 Kings 18:4; Song of Solomon 2:14

JONAH

—❦—

1:5 On What Kind of Boat Did Jonah Sail Away?

In Hebrew, the most-used term for "boat" is *oniyyah*, which the author of Jonah used to describe the ship on which the reluctant prophet gained passage. In Jonah 1:5, the author used an additional term—*sephinah*—to describe the ship. *Sephinah*, a unique word, appears only here in the Bible. Scholars believe it's a word borrowed from the Aramaic to describe a boat large enough to include a deck or a hold.[1] This makes sense in light of the fact that the sailors had to go down into the hold of the boat in order to rouse Jonah.

Tougher and larger than other vessels, a *sephinah* took merchants and sailors safely through longer, more perilous sea routes. According to early church tradition, Tarshish, the final destination for Jonah's ship, was located about two thousand miles from Joppa in southern Spain. *Tarshish* was also a generic word used to describe various ports that dotted the Mediterranean Sea, much like the word "Portland" in the United States. Wherever it was headed, the vessel that carried Jonah clearly would have been hearty enough to sustain wind, storms, and formidable waves. Perhaps this was why the seasoned sailors were especially perturbed: they had experienced storms before but never one so violent. The storm buffeted the *sephinah* so roughly that the usually strong ship "thought" to break up—the literal translation of Jonah 1:4.

1:11–15   Was Jonah Suicidal?

When Jonah instructed the scared sailors to throw him into the sea to quell the storm, did he have a death wish? Jonah 4:3 and 4:8 reiterate the prophet's desire for death, making him seem potentially suicidal. If so, his tendencies wouldn't have made him unique. The Bible includes examples of self-killing in both the Old and New Testaments. Saul committed suicide on the battlefield (1 Samuel 31:1–7). Second Samuel offers a brief description of Ahitophel's hanging (2 Samuel 17:23). And Matthew includes the account of Judas' suicide (Matthew 27:3–5).[2] The Bible gives a historical recounting of these events, without editorial comment. However, Scripture is clear about the sanctity of life and the sin of murder (Exodus 20:13; Deuteronomy 5:17).

So was Jonah, God's chosen prophet, suicidal? The Bible doesn't reveal the motive behind Jonah's words. Perhaps he was; perhaps he wasn't. The Bible does reveal *God's* view on the issue. Consider the final words of the book, God's query to the prophet: "Should I not have compassion?" Where Jonah constantly chased death and condemnation of himself, the sailors, and Nineveh, God pursued, sought, and saved all of them. God set the example to *choose life*.

Related passages: Judges 9:50–57; 1 Kings 16:15–20

1:17   A Whale of a Tale

"Jonah and the whale" is a ubiquitous description for the book of Jonah, though the Bible includes no actual mention of a "whale," only a "big fish," and the point of the book has little to do with the creature's belly. Even so, the fish-swallows-man, fish-vomits-man-out, man-continues-to-live feature is hard to ignore. Was the Mediterranean Sea near the port of Joppa really teeming with fish large enough to swallow an entire man?

Big fish were spotted on occasion along the Mediterranean coast. In fact, Mediterranean lore says that under Roman occupation, the

Joppa—or modern-day Jaffa—still supports a modest port.

port of Joppa (modern-day Jaffa) displayed a well-known mythical "sea monster," which Perseus slayed in order to rescue Andromeda. [3] The "monster's" remains are said to have had the characteristics of a sperm whale. While Perseus and Andromeda lived only in Greek mythology, sperm whales—huge, toothed whales with characteristically large mouths—most certainly could be spotted at Joppa's port in ancient times. And sperm whales are among the few sea creatures (though they are mammals, not fish) capable of swallowing a man whole. Modern accounts of humans surviving being swallowed by whale sharks also exist.

Related passage: Matthew 12:40

3:3–4 How Far Is Three Days?

In the ancient Near East, walking was one of the most practical and common modes of transportation. Long before pedometers, the average person got his or her daily steps in by fetching water, herding cattle, peddling merchandise, and even, as was the case with Jonah, by itinerant preaching.

"X number of days' walk," to the ancient listener, handily described the requisite exertion and estimated size of an area in the same way that "X miles wide" helps us imagine the breadth of a place. A day's walk was equal to the average amount of miles that a person could reasonably cover during daylight hours—about twenty miles per day. In the book of Jonah, however, "three days' walk" is more complicated, because while ancient texts approximate Nineveh's size at "four hundred and eighty stades" or fifty-five miles,[4] modern excavators of Nineveh's ruins don't measure the city as nearly sixty miles across. One explanation is that Nineveh could have been considered a representative of the whole of Assyria, which had four kingdoms. Or the phrase "three days' walk" could alternatively refer to the three days' time it customarily took to conduct official visits.[5]

Related passages: Genesis 30:36; 31:23; Exodus 3:18; Numbers 10:33; 33:8; Deuteronomy 1:2; Luke 2:44

MICAH

—✼—

1:10–15   Micah's Play on Words

Micah's rhetorical skill augments his prophecies, but much of his Hebrew wordplay gets lost in translation. A careful examination of the text reveals a skillful use of sound, irony, and double entendre. Take for example Micah 1:10–15, where the prophet customized each town's fate to fit its name. [1]

Tell it not in Gath, / Weep not at all (Micah 1:10): "In Gath," *ba gat*, has consonant sounds similar to the verb for "tell it," *tagidu*.

At Beth-le-aphrah roll yourself in the dust (1:10): Beth-le-aphrah means "house of dust."

Go on your way, inhabitant of Shaphir, in shameful nakedness (1:11): *Shaphir* means "beautiful," but the town Shaphir would be stripped and shamed. Additionally, the words for "inhabitant"— *yoshevet*—and "shame"—*boshet*—sound strikingly similar.

The inhabitant of Zaanan does not escape (1:11): The verb for "escape" or "bring out" is *yatzah*, while the word for "Zaanan" shares a similar sound—*tzanan*.

The lamentation of Beth-ezel: "He will take from you its support" (1:11): Beth-ezel means "house of nearness" or "house of proximity."

For the inhabitant of Maroth / Becomes weak waiting for good, / Because a calamity has come down from the LORD / To the gate of Jerusalem (1:12): Maroth is similar to the Hebrew word *marah*, meaning bitter. The Hebrew construction sets a clear contrast between "waiting for good"—*ki halah l tov*—and "calamity coming" instead—*ki yarad ra*.

Harness the chariot to the team of horses, / O inhabitant of Lachish (Micah 1:13): Lachish (*lakish*) sounds similar to the word for "steeds"—*rekesh*.

The houses of Achzib will become a deception / To the kings of Israel (1:14): Achzib (*akhziv*), which means "place on the dried up river," echoes the sound for the verb "deception" (*akhzav*). Deception can be vocalized alternatively to mean "dried up well" from the root verb *kzv*.

Moreover, I will bring on you / The one who takes possession, / O inhabitant of Mareshah (1:15): Mareshah sounds like the Hebrew word for conqueror, *hayoresh*. The "one who takes possession" would be like a conqueror to Mareshah. [2]

2:1   Whoa, "Woe"

The Hebrew language includes two primary words for "woe": *oy* and *hoy*. *Oy* occurs twenty-two times in the Old Testament, [3] while *hoy* occurs more than fifty times. [4] In general, the Old Testament prophets used the word *hoy* to say "ah," "ho," "alas," and "ha," (Isaiah 55:1; Jeremiah 47:6; Amos 5:18). [5] In addition, *hoy* was used as an interjection of mourning—"alas" (1 Kings 13:30; Jeremiah 22:18). In contrast, *oy* is translated "woe" almost every time it appears, with one exception (Numbers 24:23).

Used *exclusively* by the prophets to communicate impending doom, both *hoy-lak* and *oy-lak* ("woe to you!") invoked dire prophecies addressed to the unquestionably guilty. The word *woe* appears in "contexts of accusation and threat, and the mood is one of scorn and criticism." [6] In other words, these pronouncements are devoid of sympathy. Such is the case in Micah 2, which employs the word *hoy* to address the greedy who steal the livelihood and inheritance of the innocent (Micah 2:1–2).

Related passages: Numbers 21:29; 1 Samuel 4:7; Proverbs 23:29; Isaiah 24:16; Jeremiah 4:13; 22:13; Ezekiel 16:23; Hosea 9:12; Nahum 3:1; Habakkuk 2:12; Zephaniah 2:5

5:14   Around the Asherim

Asherah was one of the major goddesses in the Canaanite pantheon. The Canaanites—along with many Israelites—worshiped and made sacrifices to Asherah, because she was the goddess of fertility, the mother or consort of Baal and wife of the supreme Canaanite deity, El. [7] Shrines to Asherah consisted of groves, green trees, or wooden poles—referred to as Asherah poles or *asherim*—where lewd rituals associated with fertility took place. Eventually, *asherim* became a catch-all phrase to describe both the poles and their function.

As followers of Yahweh, Israelites were forbidden to construct such shrines and, in fact, were instructed to tear down any and every totem relating to a false god (Deuteronomy 12:3; Judges 6:25, 28, 30). However, the people of God remained enslaved to idolatry (1 Kings 14:23; Jeremiah 17:2), and Micah prophesied about a future day—still to come—when Yahweh will free His people from false idols and impotent sources of deliverance.

Related passages: Exodus 34:13; Deuteronomy 16:21; Judges 3:7;
1 Kings 14:15; 2 Chronicles 15:16; 34:3–4, 17

7:1 Fruit Pickers and Grape Gatherers

Micah lamented that, like a fruit picker or a grape gatherer after harvest, his craving for fresh fruit could not be sated because none could

Israel's vineyards should never have been completely barren, according to God's Law.

be found. His lament expressed more than just a "Who took the last cookie?" sentiment, although the longing and disappointment associated with unsated desire is certainly present. More importantly, however, Micah's woe implicated the people of Israel in wrongdoing, for in Israel, no field or vineyard should ever have been so barren that fruit pickers and grape gatherers could not glean any fruit. In order to provide for the widow, the orphan, the poor, and the foreign, the Lord had incorporated agrarian generosity into Mosaic Law, rendering it immoral to harvest twice (Leviticus 19:9–10; 23:22; Deuteronomy 24:19–22). In Micah's metaphor, the fields were barren, and the prophet was left wanting because of disobedience to God's Law. [8]

Just as the fields were bereft of fruit, the godly were nowhere to be seen in Israel. The Lord Himself longed to see the ripe fruit of righteousness in His people, and He expressed His disappointment through Micah's prophecy. The people had become dexterous at doing evil (Micah 7:3), producing briars and thorns instead of righteousness (7:4).

NAHUM

3:8   The Home of a Foreign God

No-Amon, also called Thebes, was an ancient capital of Egypt. The city, once located in Upper Egypt, stood as one of the most majestic in the ancient world, containing one hundred gates. The great river Nile ran through the heart of the city. Nahum, in his vision against Nineveh, asked if Nineveh believed itself greater than Thebes—the picture of worldly strength with its impenetrable location and powerful allies, a picture which Nahum described as having been dashed to pieces and bound in fetters (Nahum 3:10). Indeed, the city weakened as Egyptian leaders

The city of Thebes used to be a symbol of wealth and power.

chose to rule from cities much farther north in the country. Less attention from the king meant fewer resources and less power. Thebes' ultimate low point came in the seventh century BC, when the Assyrian army conquered the city. The city's ruins lie within the borders of modern-day Luxor, Egypt.

Chief among Thebes' features was its worship of the Egyptian god Amon. Some older Bible translations render the *Amon* portion of "No-Amon" in a literal sense, using terms such as "populous" or "multitudes" to highlight Thebes' great size. However, *Amon* is more appropriate, due to its being the name of the primary god worshiped there. Usually, the god Amon was portrayed with the head of a ram and the body of a man. However, as Thebes grew in national prominence, so did the fame of its god. People attributed Thebes' success to Amon and, therefore, began to associate Amon with the chief deity in other Egyptian nations—the sun god Ra. The result was a new king of the gods: Amon-Ra or Amon-Re.

Related passages: Jeremiah 46:25; Ezekiel 30:14—16

HABAKKUK

1:15–16   Fishers of Men

Habakkuk used fishing imagery to depict what was happening to God's people at the hands of the Babylonians. The prophet began by describing the wicked as swallowing the righteous—like big fish swallowing small fish (Habakkuk 1:13). But he quickly transitioned to common fishermen's tools, such as hooks and nets (1:15–16). Habakkuk made use of this imagery, not simply for the potent image of helplessness but also because these tools were the very tools the Babylonians used to capture those they conquered.

The Assyrians preceded the Babylonians in these methods. Both groups drove hooks through the lips of conquered people in order to drag them off to slavery in foreign lands. Babylonian reliefs depict foreign gods joining together to carry off large groups of people in extensive dragnets, which were like nets but let down from fishing boats on the water rather than used from the shore. Habakkuk's reference to the Babylonians offering sacrifices to their nets and burning incense to their even larger dragnets doesn't indicate that the Babylonians literally worshiped their fishing tools. Rather, Habakkuk's reference suggests that the Babylonians prided themselves in their self-reliance and put their faith in their weaponry to bring them success.

Related passages: Lamentations 1:13; Ezekiel 12:13; 19:8–9

2:6   Taunt-amount to Mockery

Ridicule has always been a fact of life in our fallen world; broken and overrun people taunt those who stumble. In the Bible, a taunt often carries with it the idea of a jesting song—such as one might hear in a military barracks. Imagine a formerly oppressed people singing in triumph as their former occupier is expelled. No longer in slavery, the downtrodden people lift their voices in celebration and direct some of their words toward the wicked oppressors of their recent past. In Deuteronomy, the Lord used this very image as a warning to the people of Israel—do not disobey lest you become an object of taunting to your former enslavers, the Egyptians (Deuteronomy 28:37).

A jesting song did not need to feature extensive lyrical content or instruments. Rather, such songs were probably brief, repetitive chants. In fact, the word Habakkuk used for "taunt-song" can also be translated simply as "proverb" or "parable," as in Ezekiel 12:23 and 24:3. We find this shortened form in Habakkuk 2:6 as well, where the entire content of the taunt-song is the statement of woe at the end of the verse—a mere nine words in Hebrew.

Related passages: Isaiah 14:4; Micah 2:4

2:19   Overlaid with Gold and Silver

Idolatry dominated the ancient world. Fashioning idols through carving or casting was common practice in virtually every city. Idols adorned people's homes and their worship spaces. And ancient people believed idols themselves were deities or at least representations of divine beings. This meant idols were treated in special ways, with offerings made to them as to gods.

Idols were generally made out of wood or metal. Isaiah offered a devastating portrait of idolatry—one that clearly shows the active role each individual played in fashioning his or her own god (Isaiah 44:9–20). Jeremiah included a similar portrait in his proclamation, making clear that idolaters took wood from the forest and decorated it themselves with silver and gold (Jeremiah 10:4). This process involved carving or casting

A woman applies gold leaf to souvenirs. The process is still in use at the King Galon gold workshop in Mandalay.

the idol, then taking a thin layer of precious metal, applying an adhesive, and lightly pounding the metal onto the idol until a thin layer slid into the crevices of the carved idol. Overlaying a lesser material with a more expensive material was common practice in the ancient world, both in the construction of idols and elsewhere.

ZEPHANIAH

—❦—

1:9 What's Wrong with a Little Leaping?

Through Zephaniah, God listed specific sinners who will be called to account on the Day of the Lord, including those who leap on the temple threshold. This pagan practice finds its origins in 1 Samuel 5. At that time, the Philistines had captured the ark of the covenant and placed it next to the idol Dagon in his temple (1 Samuel 5:2). Afterward, each time they returned, they found Dagon prostrate or in pieces before the ark. In response, the Philistines began leaping over the temple threshold to honor their fallen god, instead of walking directly upon it (5:5).

By Zephaniah's day, every aspect of life in Judah had been drenched in syncretism—the people's attempt to combine God's ways with those of foreign nations. From the dress of their leaders (Zephaniah 1:8) to the oaths of the people (1:5), Judah was unfaithful. Leaping on the temple threshold further revealed that they had placed Yahweh *beside* idols instead of His rightful position—alone.

Related passages: Exodus 20:3; Deuteronomy 6:13–15; Jeremiah 19:4–5

1:10 A "Fish Gate" and a "Second Quarter"?

The Fish Gate, also known as the First Gate,[1] was a busy thoroughfare named for the fishermen who entered Jerusalem with their daily catches from the Jordan River to sell them at the market. Interestingly, as an opening in Jerusalem's northern wall, the Fish Gate was likely where the Babylonian king Nebuchadnezzar initiated his invasion.[2] Situated north-west from Jerusalem's temple, Second Quarter, also referred to as

The Fish Gate stood in the area of the modern Damascus Gate.

New Quarter or New District, may have been the wealthy neighborhood.[3] In Zephaniah's day, it was more newly renovated than other areas.

"Fish Gate" and "Second Quarter" were as ubiquitous to Zephaniah's audience as "Wall Street" or "Beverly Hills" to readers today. God included them in Zephaniah's prophecy to point out that those who put their security in money (Zephaniah 1:11) were no match for His recompense (1:13).

Related passages: 2 Kings 22:14; 2 Chronicles 33:14; 34:22; Nehemiah 3:3; 12:39

3:14 What's All the Shouting About?

In ancient Israel, shouting was a common reaction to joy, grief, or attack. In particular, shouting was a response to circumstances that warranted faith — war, harvest, or repentance, for example. The people's shouts indicated that they trusted the Lord for protection and provision. In Zephaniah 3:14, shouting bore double significance — the loud cries signified the overflow of joy in Israel and the unequivocal victory of the faithful remnant who found refuge in the Lord.

The Lord dictated in Numbers 10:9–10 that the priests blow trumpets to assemble the people, so they would "be remembered before the LORD" during war and their offerings would remind God of His people. When the trumpet blasted, the people shouted (Joshua 6:20; 1 Chronicles 15:28; Psalm 98:6). By Zephaniah's day, the priests had lost their grip on when to blow the trumpet to demonstrate their dependence on God (Zephaniah 3:4). But God, in His mercy, remembered His people, and a righteous remnant responded to His deliverance.

Related passages: Judges 7:18; Psalm 47:5

3:17–18   The Sound of Love

In Zephaniah 3:14, God invited the people to shout for joy; in 3:17, He responded with His own shout. As the triumphant warrior, God shouted for joy over those whom He had protected as a demonstration of His zealous love. The call and response created a triumph song.

The triumph song has roots in the exodus, when Moses, Miriam, and the sons and daughters of Israel sang after God's people crossed the Red Sea (Exodus 15:1–21). When Deborah and Barak triumphed in battle, they sang about it (Judges 5). And after David felled Goliath, a song was in order (1 Samuel 18:7). Songs were so characteristic of Israel that the "songs of Zion" were internationally known (Psalm 137:3), and King David had a 288-person choir.[4]

But *God's* personal, delighted shout for joy in Zephaniah 3:17 is extraordinary in the Bible. The word for "love" here is *ahabah*, a term that typically denotes singular, even doting, devotion when used by God, as in Isaiah 63:9, Jeremiah 31:3, and Hosea 11:4. In addition, *ahabah* indicates deep friendship in 1 Samuel 18:3, as well as romantic love in Proverbs 5:19 and Song of Solomon 2:4–5.

Related passages: Psalm 66:1; 100:1–2; Ecclesiastes 9:6

HAGGAI

2:12 The Food of Sacrifice

In Moses' day, the Lord gave His people directions for worship—both for constructing a worship space (the tabernacle—and later the temple) as well as for worshiping within that space. A number of the worship regulations involved people bringing sacrifices. Some sacrifices called for grain and flour, but many demanded animals.

The process of making an offering involved an individual choosing an animal—such as a goat, sheep, or cow—in excellent condition and taking it to the priest to sacrifice on his or her behalf. The priests

Priests would sacrifice unblemished goats to worship God in Moses' day.

had means to cook the animal on site and, once finished, would take a portion outlined by the Mosaic Law for their livelihood. Offerings occurred at certain times of year designated for making sacrifices and at other times for other reasons such as sin. The Lord deemed these sacrifices holy, because of the context in which they were offered (Leviticus 6:24–26).

Priests and others avoided touching the sacrificed meat out of appreciation for the distinction between God's holiness and their own fallen status (Haggai 2:12). Therefore, priests ate the meat within the tabernacle, while individuals took the remains of their sacrifices home in the folds of their garments. This was in accordance with the Levitical directions to wash (or destroy) whatever came into contact with the meat (Leviticus 6:27–28). God directed the people in this way to remind them of their fallen natures and their need to take care to pursue holiness. This would be a special meal, set apart from all others—thus people took special care before consuming it.

Related passages: Exodus 29:31–34; Leviticus 2:1–11; Jeremiah 11:15

ZECHARIAH

—❈—

1:7–11 Earth Patrol

Zechariah prophesied to Jewish exiles making their way back home with the blessing of Persia. The prophet first referenced Persia in chapter 1, verse 1, where he marked time by the reign of King Darius—the Persian Empire's greatest king. One of Darius' predecessors described Persia as "a land of fine horses and good men."[1] The Persian monarchy utilized both in order to supervise and secure the vast regions of the kingdom. It wasn't unusual for regions to have surprise visits from "the ears of the king"—tax officials or military officers who ensured that each satrapy behaved in accordance with the empire.[2]

In Zechariah 1, the Lord appropriated the Persian patrolling practice to communicate the supremacy of His watchful control as well as the vastness of His kingdom. Zechariah's imagery of horsemen patrolling the earth would have reminded apt listeners that God's providence is greater than the most powerful earthly kingdom and His watchful eye would not leave Jerusalem vulnerable forever (Zechariah 1:15–17).

Related passage: Revelation 6

2:8 The Apple of God's Eye

A well-known English idiom, "apple of the eye" refers to a person or thing that is treasured or favored. The expression originated in the King James translation of Deuteronomy 32:10, which Zechariah 2:8 echoes. Interestingly, although the King James uses "apple" in both places, the actual Hebrew terms differ significantly. Deuteronomy 32:10 uses *ishon*,[3] meaning "little man," while Zechariah employs *bavah*,[4]

127

The "apple" of God's eye isn't about fruit.

meaning "gate." Both verses describe an aspect of the eye. The reflection in the eye of a beheld person looks like a miniature, and the pupil can be considered the gate of the eye. Both *ishon* and *bavah* describe the vulnerability and focus of the eye—that aspect of the "apple of the eye" expression remains intact in its accuracy.

In Zechariah, God communicated that hurting Zion is like poking God in the eye—a provocative, foolish endeavor. Some scholars assert that the reference foreshadows Christ's being sent against "the nations" for plundering His people.[5] The New Testament bears witness to Jesus' zeal to not only protect the most vulnerable of those who believe in Him but to also regard their suffering as His own (Matthew 25:34–45).

Related passages: Psalm 17:8; Proverbs 7:2; Acts 9:1, 4–5

3:4   Festal Robes

Festal robes signified holiness. In ancient Israel, this special garb was donned only on special occasions—it was set apart. Similar to our "Sunday best" or formal gala attire, the festal robes—*mahalasa* in

Hebrew, meaning "robe of state"[6]—were distinguished from everyday apparel and represented the purity and wealth of the wearer.

Two instances of "festal robe" in the prophetic books serve as a comparative study of pride and humility. In Isaiah 3:22, the Lord took the festal robes from the daughters of Zion because of their pride and mistreatment of the poor; He replaced the robes with sackcloth and rope—the garments of slavery. In contrast, in Zechariah 3:4, the Lord rewarded Joshua first by taking away filthy garments that were similar to slavery garb, then clothing him with festal robes. These were not robes Joshua could have obtained himself; they were gifts from the Lord, symbolizing the fact that God chose Jerusalem to represent Him as a priestly nation.

8:19 Fasts? What Fasts?

Mosaic Law prescribed only one fast: the Day of Atonement (Leviticus 23:27–32). The solemn fasts practiced during Judah's captivity and mentioned in Zechariah 8:19 served memorial purposes only. These included:

- **The fast of the fourth month**—observed during the month of Tammuz as a memorial of the breach of Jerusalem's walls, followed by the capture of Judah's King Zedekiah in 586 BC (Jeremiah 39:1–5)[7]

- **The fast of the fifth month**—observed in the month of Av to commemorate Nebuchadnezzar's burning of Solomon's temple in 586 BC (2 Kings 25:8)[8]

- **The fast of the seventh month**—observed in the month of Tishri to commemorate the murder of Judah's governor Gedaliah (Jeremiah 41:1–2) around 581 BC[9]

- **The fast of the tenth month**—observed during the month of Tevet to remember the beginning of Babylon's siege against Jerusalem (2 Kings 25:1)[10]

Sadly, the people did not perform these self-instituted fasts in pious commemoration; instead, the fasts became disingenuous affectations (Zechariah 7:3–6). Nonetheless, the Lord promised to turn Judah's fasts into times of feasting (8:19).

Related passage: Isaiah 58:4

9:1 Where Is Hadrach?

Hadrach is somewhat of a biblical anomaly: Bible readers won't find the name of this place anywhere except in Zechariah 9:1, and not even there in some translations (like NLT). Because Zechariah mentioned Hadrach right before Damascus, scholars hypothesize that the land was located to the north, since Zechariah's list seems to list cities by location, beginning in the north and moving southward to Sidon.[11] Scholars have also unearthed evidence that Hadrach might have been a city cited in Assyrian logs: Hatarikka. "Tiglath-pileser III named 'the city of Hatarikka' in his annals as one of the 'nineteen districts of Hamath' that had gone over to support Azariah of Judah."[12] If Hatarikka was in view, its location began near Aleppo.

10:2 Teraphim

Teraphim is a Hebrew term meaning "idols" or "images."[13] When not directly transliterated, it is most commonly translated as "household idols." Teraphim, unfortunately, appear frequently in every epoch of the Old Testament, usually as a means of divination (2 Kings 23:24; Ezekiel 21:21). Household idols were also linked to ancestor worship, which may have been Rachel's motivation for absconding with her father's idols in Genesis 31:19. Although teraphim are usually thought to have been portable, 1 Samuel 19:12–16 depicts them as large enough to be mistaken for David.

To God, the ubiquitous presence of teraphim among His people, even during the post-exilic period of Zechariah's prophecies, reeked with the constant stench of unfaithfulness and fear that characterized those whom He had set apart to be a royal priesthood. Rather than humbly seeking God for provision (Zechariah 10:1), Israel had relied on pagan rites. Out of compassion, the Lord desired to punish those who misled His people and provide them with a worthy Shepherd (10:2).

Related passages: Genesis 31:34–35; Judges 17:5; 18:14, 17–20; 1 Samuel 15:23; Hosea 3:4

12:11   Mourning Like Who . . . or What?

The difficult Hebrew construction of the phrase "like the mourning of Hadadrimmon" has divided scholars as to its meaning—a meaning that hangs on a simple preposition. Two main camps of interpretation can easily be observed in English translations. The first camp—including the NIV, NASB, KJV, and NLT—translates the phrase as "mourning

Hadadrimmon may have been located here, near the Valley of Jezreel.

of Hadadrimmon." The second camp—including the CEV, NCV, and NRSV—translates it as "mourning *for* Hadadrimmon." [14]

The first camp's rendering presumes Hadadrimmon is a *place*, specifically, a hamlet near Jezreel in the Megiddo plain, where Josiah, righteous king of Judah, was murdered by Egypt's Pharaoh Neco II (2 Chronicles 35:20–27). [15] The second camp's interpretation intimates that Hadadrimmon is a *person*—a combination of two Canaanite gods. Hadad was the god of the storm; Rimmon ruled thunder. [16] If the second camp is correct, it would be unusual for Yahweh to compare "Me who they have pierced" (Zechariah 12:10)—a foreshadowing of Jesus—to pagan gods. Perhaps if this interpretation is accurate, God was instead comparing righteous mourning with the idolatrous grieving the Israelites formerly practiced.

13:6   Wounds Between the Arms

One of the marks of an Old Testament false prophet was skin-deep—they would cut themselves to provoke a divine response (1 Kings 18:28) or mourn the dead (Jeremiah 16:6). This behavior was in direct opposition to God's Law (Leviticus 19:28; 21:5). Therefore, during the period when God refines His people so only the righteous remnant remain, those who value their lives will no longer prophesy apart from God's leading.

Ambiguous in Hebrew, the phrase "between the arms" in Zechariah 13 literally reads, "between your hands." Some scholars think the phrase refers to cuts on the back, while others think it refers to cuts upon the chest. [17] In either case, when the day of judgment comes, false prophets will attribute their wounds to clumsiness or abuse rather than divination because their fear of the Lord will be so great.

Related passages: Jeremiah 41:5; 48:37

The Mount of Olives

14:4   The Mount of Olives

Readers should not miss the eschatological significance of Zechariah 14:4—one of only two places in the Old Testament that refers to the "Mount of Olives" (2 Samuel 15:30). Zechariah's reference provides a prophetic link to the messianic activity described in the New Testament.

Zechariah described the day when the Lord will defend Jerusalem against the nations that threaten it. On that day, the Lord "will stand on the Mount of Olives" as the ultimate Deliverer (Zechariah 14:4). As a result, the Mount of Olives is intimately associated with the life and ministry of Jesus. Jesus frequented the Mount of Olives to teach (Matthew 24:3–25), view Jerusalem, triumphantly enter the city (Mark 11:1–10), and weep and pray before His betrayal (Luke 22:39–48). Second Samuel 15:30 refers to the "ascent of the Mount of Olives," where David, the Messiah's forebear, wept as he fled his son Absalom. Just as David wept and worshiped, so did the Son of David.

The Mount of Olives was the last place Jesus stood before He ascended into heaven (Acts 1:9–12), and Revelation 19:11–21 portends the time when His feet will once again tread there. This passage echoes the day of the Lord, when He will descend with His holy ones to war with the nations, whom the Lord will defeat forever, establishing His name as "the only one" (Zechariah 14:3–9; Revelation 19:14–16). [18]

Related passages: Matthew 24–25

MALACHI

1:7 Spoiled Sacrifices

Malachi's ministry dates to the time period following Judah's return from captivity in Babylon. After Ezra the priest led in the temple rebuilding project and Nehemiah raised strong walls to protect Jerusalem, God's priests sought to reestablish the sacrificial system that had been neglected while God's people lived as exiles in Babylon.

Through the prophet Malachi, God condemned His priests for making sacrifices with defiled animals—those that were not ritually clean. Mosaic Law gave specific instructions on what God considered acceptable sacrifices—flawless, male bulls, sheep, and goats without blemish. God would not accept blind animals or those with broken bones or skin conditions (Leviticus 22:17–25). The priests in Malachi's day didn't fear the Lord, so they didn't select their sacrifices with care. Their worship amounted to empty ritual, and their blemished sacrifices defiled the altar and mocked God.

Related passages: Exodus 29:1; Deuteronomy 17:1; Ezekiel 43:22–25

1:12 God's Dinner Table

When Malachi used the word *food* to describe priests' sacrifices and *table* to describe the altar in the temple, he was employing human analogies to help the people understand the priests' acts as part of their covenant with God. Then and now, in order for people to live in relationship with God, they must come to Him on His terms and receive cleansing for their sin. Believers today put their faith in Jesus Christ's sacrifice in order to enter into relationship with God. In Old Testament times, people still came to God through faith, but they relied on priests to facilitate their relationship through sacrifices. The "table of the Lord" in Malachi 1:12 probably refers to all the sacrifices the priests offered. Alternatively, it could indicate the altar of burnt offering mentioned in 1:7. Either way, God expected priests to conduct their duties with fear and reverence.

This covenant relationship looked a lot like another one in the ancient Near East — the one between a king and his vassal. When a victorious king, or suzerain, conquered another nation or territory, he often made the conquered ruler his vassal, or servant. A vassal paid taxes to his suzerain and swore allegiance to him. The covenant relationship between the suzerain and the vassal was ratified over a meal.[1]

The Old Testament's food and table imagery continued through the New Testament with the communion table, which represents the relationship Christians enjoy with God through Christ's sacrificial death and victorious resurrection. In 1 Corinthians 10:16 – 22, Paul reminded

Replica of altar of burnt offerings at reconstructed tabernacle, Timna Park, Israel

believers to remain pure and fear the Lord so that when they come to the His table, they won't be found guilty—but will partake in a worthy manner.

Related passages: Leviticus 21:6; Hebrews 9:2

3:5   Care for Orphans

In Old Testament times, orphans were those without fathers and, therefore, without legal standing in the covenant community. Throughout Scripture, God revealed His regard for orphans and gave explicit instruction for their care. In Exodus 22:21–24, God promised to protect and provide for widows, orphans, and strangers. In Deuteronomy 26:12–13, Moses instructed God's people to give a tithe every third year for the Levites, strangers, orphans, and widows. The psalms portray God as the "father of the fatherless" (Psalm 68:5) and the defender of orphans (82:3). The prophets also reminded God's people of the Lord's compassion toward the fatherless and His expectation that His people would also show them compassion (Ezekiel 22:6–7). And in Malachi, God promised to judge His people for neglecting orphans. In fact, He grouped together those who neglected orphans with sorcerers, adulterers, and liars.

Other ancient Near Eastern nations also expected their rulers and citizens to care for orphans. Three important Mesopotamian legal codes, including the famous Law of Hammurabi in the eighteenth century BC, explained the importance of caring for orphans and pursuing justice on their behalf. In ancient Egypt, kings often boasted of their generosity toward orphans, widows, and the poor.[2]

Related passages: Deuteronomy 10:18; Psalm 10:17–18; James 1:27

3:16   Book of Remembrance

Time and again, God spoke reproof to His people through Malachi. Some of the prophet's audience took God's severe admonition to heart. The faithful few repented. The "book of remembrance," mentioned only in Malachi 3:16, was either their written, signed commitment to obey God[3] or a record of their faithfulness, kept by God in heaven.[4]

The "book of remembrance" may be related to the "book of life" in which the names of the righteous appear. In Psalm 69:28, David asked God to erase from the book of life those who had rejected and tried to kill him, a metaphor for judgment. But Revelation 13:8 assures believers that their deliverance from God's judgment is guaranteed, for their names were written in the book of the life "from the foundation of the world." Malachi 3:17 includes a reference to the coming "day of the Lord," in which God will "spare" the righteous and judge those who have rejected His provision of grace, ultimately displayed in Jesus Christ. Whether the book of remembrance and the book of life are one in the same, and whether the faithful remnant in Malachi's day wrote their own "book of remembrance" or God has kept the book in heaven, they most assuredly will be spared on the coming day of judgment.

Related passages: Philippians 4:3; Revelation 3:5; 20:12–15

APPENDIX

TIMELINE OF OLD TESTAMENT BOOKS AND EVENTS

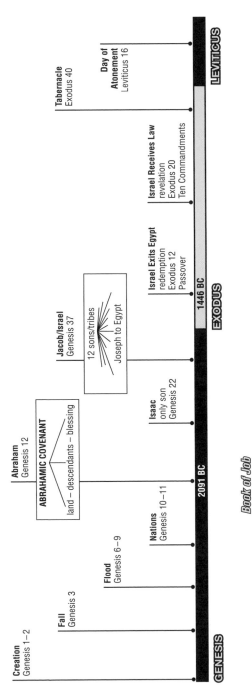

Creation
Genesis 1–2

Fall
Genesis 3

Flood
Genesis 6–9

Nations
Genesis 10–11

Abraham
Genesis 12

ABRAHAMIC COVENANT
land – descendants – blessing

Isaac
only son
Genesis 22

Jacob/Israel
Genesis 37

12 sons/tribes

Joseph to Egypt

Israel Exits Egypt
redemption
Exodus 12
Passover

Israel Receives Law
revelation
Exodus 20
Ten Commandments

Tabernacle
Exodus 40

Day of Atonement
Leviticus 16

GENESIS

2091 BC

1446 BC

EXODUS

LEVITICUS

Book of Job

Legend: PENTATEUCH • HISTORICAL BOOKS • *Wisdom Books* • *Prophetical Books*

TIMELINE OF OLD TESTAMENT BOOKS AND EVENTS, CONT.

UNITED KINGDOM →

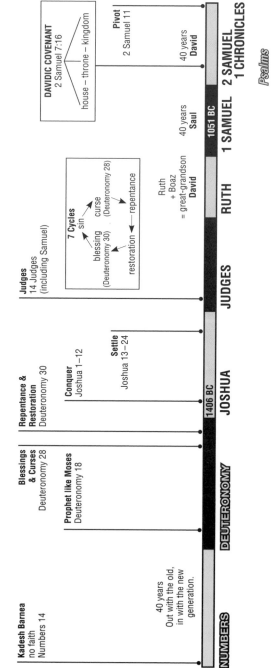

Kadesh Barnea
no faith
Numbers 14

40 years
Out with the old,
in with the new
generation.

NUMBERS

Blessings & Curses
Deuteronomy 28

Prophet like Moses
Deuteronomy 18

DEUTERONOMY

Repentance & Restoration
Deuteronomy 30

Conquer
Joshua 1–12

Settle
Joshua 13–24

1406 BC

JOSHUA

Judges
14 Judges
(including Samuel)

7 Cycles
sin
blessing → curse
(Deuteronomy 30) (Deuteronomy 28)
restoration ← repentance

Ruth
+ Boaz
= great-grandson
David

JUDGES

RUTH

DAVIDIC COVENANT
2 Samuel 7:16
house – throne – kingdom

Pivot
2 Samuel 11

40 years
David

40 years
Saul

1051 BC

1 SAMUEL

2 SAMUEL
1 CHRONICLES

Psalms

TIMELINE OF OLD TESTAMENT BOOKS AND EVENTS, CONT.

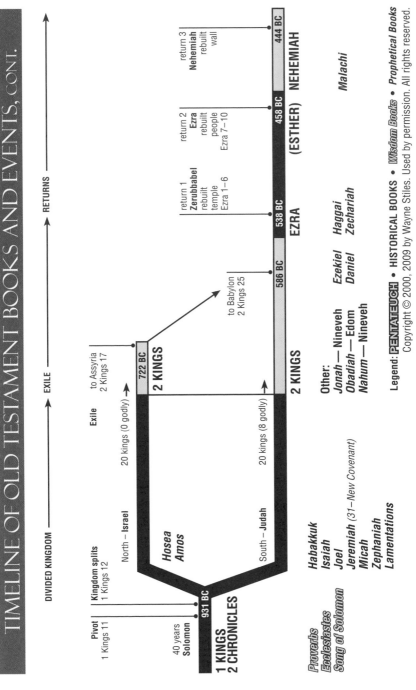

DIVIDED KINGDOM → EXILE → RETURNS →

Pivot
1 Kings 11

Kingdom splits
1 Kings 12

Exile

to Assyria
2 Kings 17

40 years
Solomon

931 BC

North – **Israel**

20 kings (0 godly)

South – **Judah**

20 kings (8 godly)

722 BC

2 KINGS

to Babylon
2 Kings 25

586 BC

2 KINGS

return 1
Zerubbabel
rebuilt
temple
Ezra 1–6

538 BC

EZRA

return 2
Ezra
rebuilt
people
Ezra 7–10

458 BC

(ESTHER)

return 3
Nehemiah
rebuilt
wall

444 BC

NEHEMIAH

Hosea
Amos

Habakkuk
Isaiah
Joel
Jeremiah (31 – New Covenant)
Micah
Zephaniah
Lamentations

Other:
Jonah — Nineveh
Obadiah — Edom
Nahum — Nineveh

Ezekiel
Daniel

Haggai
Zechariah

Malachi

Proverbs
Ecclesiastes
Song of Solomon

1 KINGS
2 CHRONICLES

Legend: **PENTATEUCH** • **HISTORICAL BOOKS** • *Wisdom Books* • *Prophetical Books*
Copyright © 2000, 2009 by Wayne Stiles. Used by permission. All rights reserved.

143

HOW TO BEGIN A RELATIONSHIP WITH GOD

The Bible retains its relevance in all cultures and communities. The message of Scripture speaks to all people because all people have been created by God in His image, all people have fallen from the original state of glory, and all people are in need of God's salvation through Jesus. The Bible marks the path to Him with four essential truths. Let's look at each marker in detail.

Our Spiritual Condition: Totally Depraved

The first truth is rather personal. One look in the mirror of Scripture, and our human condition becomes painfully clear:

> "There is none righteous, not even one;
> There is none who understands,
> There is none who seeks for God;
> All have turned aside, together they have become useless;
> There is none who does good,
> There is not even one." (Romans 3:10–12)

We are all sinners through and through—totally depraved. Now, that doesn't mean we've committed every atrocity known to humankind. We're not as *bad* as we can be, just as *bad off* as we can be. Sin colors all our thoughts, motives, words, and actions.

If you've been around a while, you likely already believe it. Look around. Everything around us bears the smudge marks of our sinful nature. Despite our best efforts to create a perfect world, crime statistics continue to soar, divorce rates keep climbing, and families keep crumbling.

Something has gone terribly wrong in our society and in ourselves—something deadly. Contrary to how the world would repackage it, "me-first" living doesn't equal rugged individuality and freedom; it equals death. As Paul said in his letter to the Romans, "The wages of sin is death" (Romans 6:23)—our spiritual and physical death that comes from God's righteous judgment of our sin, along with all of the emotional and practical effects of this separation that we experience on a daily basis. This brings us to the second marker: God's character.

God's Character: Infinitely Holy

How can God judge us for a sinful state we were born into? Our total depravity is only half the answer. The other half is God's infinite holiness.

The fact that we know things are not as they should be points us to a standard of goodness beyond ourselves. Our sense of injustice in life on this side of eternity implies a perfect standard of justice beyond our reality. That standard and source is God Himself. And God's standard of holiness contrasts starkly with our sinful condition.

Scripture says that "God is Light, and in Him there is no darkness at all" (1 John 1:5). God is absolutely holy—which creates a problem for us. If He is so pure, how can we who are so impure relate to Him?

Perhaps we could try being better people, try to tilt the balance in favor of our good deeds, or seek out methods for self-improvement. Throughout history, people have attempted to live up to God's standard by keeping the Ten Commandments or living by their own code of ethics. Unfortunately, no one can come close to satisfying the demands of God's law. Romans 3:20 says, "By the works of the Law no flesh will be justified in His sight; for through the Law comes the knowledge of sin."

Our Need: A Substitute

So here we are, sinners by nature and sinners by choice, trying to pull ourselves up by our own bootstraps to attain a relationship with our holy Creator. But every time we try, we fall flat on our faces. We can't live a good enough life to make up for our sin, because God's standard isn't "good enough"—it's *perfection*. And we can't make amends for the offense our sin has created without dying for it.

Who can get us out of this mess?

If someone could live perfectly, honoring God's law, and would bear sin's death penalty for us—in our place—then we would be saved from our predicament. But is there such a person? Thankfully, yes!

Meet your substitute—*Jesus Christ*. He is the One who took death's place for you!

> [God] made [Jesus Christ] who knew no sin to be sin on our behalf, so that we might become the righteousness of God in Him. (2 Corinthians 5:21)

God's Provision: A Savior

God rescued us by sending His Son, Jesus, to die on the cross for our sins (1 John 4:9–10). Jesus was fully human and fully divine (John 1:1, 18), a truth that ensures His understanding of our weaknesses, His power to forgive, and His ability to bridge the gap between God and us (Romans 5:6–11). In short, we are "justified as a gift by His grace through the redemption which is in Christ Jesus" (Romans 3:24). Two words in this verse bear further explanation: *justified* and *redemption*.

Justification is God's act of mercy, in which He declares righteous the believing sinners while we are still in our sinning state. Justification doesn't mean that God *makes* us righteous, so that we never sin again, rather that He *declares* us righteous—much like a judge pardons a guilty criminal. Because Jesus took our sin upon Himself and suffered our judgment on the cross, God forgives our debt and proclaims us PARDONED.

Redemption is Christ's act of paying the complete price to release us from sin's bondage. God sent His Son to bear His wrath for all of our sins—past, present, and future (Romans 3:24–26; 2 Corinthians 5:21). In humble obedience, Christ willingly endured the shame of the cross for our sake (Mark 10:45; Romans 5:6–8; Philippians 2:8). Christ's death satisfied God's righteous demands. He no longer holds our sins against us, because His own Son paid the penalty for them. We are freed from the slave market of sin, never to be enslaved again!

Placing Your Faith in Christ

These four truths describe how God has provided a way to Himself through Jesus Christ. Because the price has been paid in full by God, we must respond to His free gift of eternal life in total faith and confidence in Him to save us. We must step forward into the relationship with God that He has prepared for us—not by doing good works or by being a good person, but by coming to Him just as we are and accepting His justification and redemption by faith.

> For by grace you have been saved through faith; and that not of yourselves, it is the gift of God; not as a result of works, so that no one may boast. (Ephesians 2:8–9)

We accept God's gift of salvation simply by placing our faith in Christ alone for the forgiveness of our sins. Would you like to enter a relationship with your Creator by trusting in Christ as your Savior? If so, here's a simple prayer you can use to express your faith:

> *Dear God,*
>
> *I know that my sin has put a barrier between You and me. Thank You for sending Your Son, Jesus, to die in my place. I trust in Jesus alone to forgive my sins, and I accept His gift of eternal life. I ask Jesus to be my personal Savior and the Lord of my life. Thank You. In Jesus' name, amen.*

If you've prayed this prayer or one like it and you wish to find out more about knowing God and His plan for you in the Bible, contact us at Insight for Living Ministries. Our contact information is on the following pages.

WE ARE HERE FOR YOU

If you desire to find out more about knowing God and His plan for you in the Bible, contact us. Insight for Living Ministries provides staff pastors who are available for free written correspondence or phone consultation. These seminary-trained and seasoned counselors have years of experience and are well-qualified guides for your spiritual journey.

Please feel welcome to contact your regional office by using the information below:

United States

Insight for Living Ministries
Biblical Counseling Department
Post Office Box 5000
Frisco, Texas 75034-0055
USA
972-473-5097 (Monday through Friday,
8:00 a.m.–5:00 p.m. central time)
www.insight.org/contactapastor

Canada

Insight for Living Canada
Biblical Counseling Department
PO Box 8 Stn A
Abbotsford BC V2T 6Z4
CANADA
1-800-663-7639
info@insightforliving.ca

Australia, New Zealand, and South Pacific

Insight for Living Australia
Pastoral Care
Post Office Box 443
Boronia, VIC 3155
AUSTRALIA
+61 3 9762 6613

United Kingdom and Europe

Insight for Living United Kingdom
Pastoral Care
PO Box 553
Dorking
RH4 9EU
UNITED KINGDOM
0800 787 9364
+44 1306 640156
www.insightforliving.org.uk

ENDNOTES

Job

1.   Roy B. Zuck, "Job," in *The Bible Knowledge Commentary: Old Testament*, ed. John F. Walvoord and Roy B. Zuck (Wheaton, Ill.: Victor Books, 1986), 718–19.

2.   J. R. Michaels, "Servant," in *The Zondervan Pictorial Encyclopedia of the Bible*, vol. 5, *Q–Z*, gen. ed. Merrill C. Tenney (Grand Rapids: Zondervan, 1976), 358–59.

3.   Zuck, "Job," in *The Bible Knowledge Commentary: Old Testament*, 723.

4.   G. S. Cansdale, "Crocodile," in *The Zondervan Pictorial Encyclopedia of the Bible*, vol. 1, *A–C*, 1037.

5.   Zuck, "Job," in *The Bible Knowledge Commentary: Old Testament*, 771–72.

6.   John Rea, "Caravan," in *The Zondervan Pictorial Encyclopedia of the Bible*, vol. 1, *A–C*, gen. ed. Merrill C. Tenney (Grand Rapids: Zondervan, 1976), 751.

7.   Zuck, "Job," in *The Bible Knowledge Commentary: Old Testament*, 727.

8.   J. I. Packer and Merrill C. Tenney, eds., "Transportation," in *Illustrated Manners and Customs of the Bible* (Nashville: Thomas Nelson, 1980), 294–95, 299.

9.   F. B. Huey, Jr., "Weaving," in *The Zondervan Pictorial Encyclopedia of the Bible*, vol. 5, *Q–Z*, 911.

10. Howard F. Vos, "Papyrus," in *The New Unger's Bible Dictionary*, ed. R. K. Harrison (Chicago: Moody Press, 1988), 959.

11. "Mineral Kingdom," in *The New Unger's Bible Dictionary*, 860–63, 866, 868, 870.

12. Merrill F. Unger, "Glass," in *The New Unger's Bible Dictionary*, 478.

13. George E. Post, "Fishing," in *The New Unger's Bible Dictionary*, 430–31.

14. Thomas L. Constable, "Notes on Numbers," 2015 ed., Sonic Light, http://soniclight.com/constable/notes/htm/OT/Numbers/Numbers.htm, note 27:1–11, accessed May 18, 2015.

Psalms

1. C. Hassell Bullock, *Encountering the Book of Psalms: A Literary and Theological Introduction* (Grand Rapids: Baker Academic, 2001), 125, 126, 131.

2. *Encountering the Book of Psalms*, 136.

3. *Encountering the Book of Psalms*, 152.

4. *Encountering the Book of Psalms*, 166.

5. *Encountering the Book of Psalms*, 178, 182–83.

6. *Encountering the Book of Psalms*, 188–89.

7. *Encountering the Book of Psalms*, 202.

8. *Encountering the Book of Psalms*, 214, 216–17.

9. *Encountering the Book of Psalms*, 228.

10. J. G. S. S. Thompson and F. D. Kidner, "Book of Psalms," in *New Bible Dictionary*, 2nd ed., ed. J. D. Douglas, and others (Wheaton, Ill.: Tyndale House, 1982), 993–94.

11. W. E. Shewell-Cooper, "Fruit (Products)," in *The Zondervan Pictorial Encyclopedia of the Bible*, vol. 2, *D–G*, ed. Merrill C. Tenney (Grand Rapids: Zondervan, 1976), 609–10.

12. D. R. Bowes, "Metals and Metallurgy," in *The Zondervan Pictorial Encyclopedia of the Bible*, vol. 4, *M–P*, ed. Merrill C. Tenney (Grand Rapids: Zondervan, 1976), 207–208, 210.

13. Merrill F. Unger, "Shepherd," in *The New Unger's Bible Dictionary*, ed. R. K. Harrison (Chicago: Moody Press, 1988), 1179–80.

14. Unger, "Anointing," in *The New Unger's Bible Dictionary*, 80–81.

15. "Clothing and Cosmetics," in *Illustrated Manners and Customs of the Bible*, ed. J. I. Packer and Merrill C. Tenney (Nashville: Thomas Nelson, 1980), 484.

16. Arthur B. Fowler, "Sheol," in *Zondervan's Pictorial Bible Dictionary*, ed. Merrill C. Tenney (Grand Rapids: Zondervan, 1967), 784.

17. "Plants and Herbs," in *Illustrated Manners and Customs of the Bible*, 252.

18. Merrill F. Unger, "Asaph," in *The New Unger's Bible Dictionary*, ed. R. K. Harrison (Chicago: Moody Press, 1988), 111.

19. Bullock, *Encountering the Book of Psalms: A Literary and Theological Introduction*, 77.

20. J. B. Payne, "Jerusalem," in *The Zondervan Pictorial Encyclopedia of the Bible*, vol. 3, *H–L*, ed. Merrill C. Tenney (Grand Rapids: Zondervan, 1976), 460, 462.

21. J. B. Payne, "Zion," in *The Zondervan Pictorial Encyclopedia of the Bible*, vol. 5, *Q–Z*, ed. Merrill C. Tenney (Grand Rapids: Zondervan, 1976), 1063, 1065.

22. J. I. Packer and Merrill C. Tenney, eds., "Plants and Herbs," in *Illustrated Manners and Customs of the Bible* (Nashville: Thomas Nelson, 1980), 256.

23. Packer and Tenney, eds., "The Animals and Insects of Palestine," in *Illustrated Manners and Customs of the Bible*, 229.

24. Thomas L. Constable, "Notes on Psalms," 2015 ed., Sonic Light, http://soniclight.com/constable/notes/pdf/psalms.pdf, note 118:22–24, accessed Nov. 3, 2015.

25. Edward Mack, "Cornerstone," in *The International Standard Bible Encyclopedia*, vol. 1, *A–D*, ed. Geoffrey W. Bromiley (Grand Rapids: Eerdmans, 1988), 784.

26. *Merriam-Webster's Collegiate Dictionary*, 11th ed. (Springfield, Mass.: Merriam-Webster, 2007), "acrostic."

27. Constable, "Notes on Psalms," note 137:8–9.

Proverbs

1.   Charles H. Dyer, "Jeremiah," in *The Bible Knowledge Commentary: Old Testament*, ed. John F. Walvoord and Roy B. Zuck (Wheaton, Ill.: Victor Books, 1986), 1132.

Ecclesiastes

1.   "Jerusalem Archaeological Sites: Biblical Water Systems," in Jewish Virtual Library, https://www.jewishvirtuallibrary.org/jsource/Archaeology/jerwater.html, accessed Aug. 10, 2015.

2.   NET Bible, "Notes on Ecclesiastes," https://lumina.bible.org/bible/Ecclesiastes+2, Eccl. 2:5, textual note 30, accessed Aug. 11, 2015.

3.   E. A. Judge, "Slave, Slavery," in *New Bible Dictionary*, 2nd ed., ed. J. D. Douglas and others (Wheaton, Ill.: Tyndale House, 1987), 1121–22.

4.   "Tools and Implements," in *Illustrated Manners and Customs of the Bible*, ed. J. I. Packer and Merrill C. Tenney (Nashville: Thomas Nelson, 1980), 272, 275–76.

5.   NET Bible, "Notes on Ecclesiastes," https://lumina.bible.org/bible/Ecclesiastes+11, Eccl. 11:1, textual note 3, accessed Aug. 12, 2015.

6. "Agriculture," in *Illustrated Manners and Customs of the Bible*, 264.

Isaiah

1. Thomas L. Constable, "Notes on Isaiah," 2015 ed., Sonic Light, http://soniclight.com/constable/notes/htm/OT/Isaiah/Isaiah.htm, note 1:4–9, accessed July 28, 2015.

2. J. S. Wright, "Day of the Lord," in *New Bible Dictionary*, 2nd ed., ed. J. D. Douglas and others (Wheaton, Ill.: Tyndale House, 1987), 269.

3. Charles R. Swindoll, *Swindoll's Living Insights: Insights on Revelation* (Wheaton, Ill.: Tyndale House, 2014), 97.

4. "Plants and Herbs," in *Illustrated Manners and Customs of the Bible*, ed. J. I. Packer and Merrill C. Tenney (Nashville: Thomas Nelson, 1980), 258.

5. Constable, "Notes on Isaiah," note 7:15–16.

6. G. I. Davies, "Dedan," in *New Bible Dictionary*, 2nd ed., 277.

7. D. J. Wiseman, "Ariel," in *New Bible Dictionary*, 2nd ed., 81.

8. "Hearth," in *Zondervan's Pictorial Bible Dictionary*, ed. Merrill C. Tenney (Grand Rapids: Zondervan, 1967), 340.

9. Wiseman, "Bel," in *New Bible Dictionary*, 2nd ed., 129.

10. Wiseman, "Merodach," in *New Bible Dictionary*, 2nd ed., 761–62.

11. Wiseman, "Nebo," in *New Bible Dictionary*, 2nd ed., 820.

Jeremiah

1. Charles H. Dyer, "Jeremiah," in *The Bible Knowledge Commentary: Old Testament*, ed. John F. Walvoord and Roy B. Zuck (Wheaton, Ill.: Victor Books, 1986), 1132.

2. Thomas L. Constable, "Notes on Jeremiah," 2015 ed., Sonic Light, http://soniclight.com/constable/notes/htm/OT/Jeremiah/Jeremiah.htm, note 2.16, accessed May 29, 2015.

3. R. L Mixter, "Hair," in *The Zondervan Pictorial Encyclopedia of the Bible*, vol. 3, *H–L*, ed. Merrill C. Tenney (Grand Rapids: Zondervan, 1976), 15–16.

4. Constable, "Notes on Jeremiah," note 7.18.

5. Merrill F. Unger, "Mourn," in *The New Unger's Bible Dictionary*, ed. R. K. Harrison (Chicago: Moody Press, 1988), 891–92; Constable, "Notes on Jeremiah," note 9.17, accessed May 29, 2015.

6.   Unger, "Seal, Signet," in *The New Unger's Bible Dictionary*, 1150 – 51.

7.   H. F. Vos, "Papyrus," in *The New Unger's Bible Dictionary*, 959 – 60;
J. N. Birdsall, "Codex," in *The Zondervan Pictorial Encyclopedia of the Bible*, vol. 1,
A – C, ed. Merrill C. Tenney (Grand Rapids: Zondervan, 1976), 898 – 99.

8.   Constable, "Notes on Jeremiah," note 37.15 – 16.

9.   C. E. De Vries, "Obelisk," in *The Zondervan Pictorial Encyclopedia of the Bible*,
vol. 4, *M – P*, ed. Merrill C. Tenney (Grand Rapids: Zondervan, 1976), 486;
Constable, "Notes on Jeremiah," note 43.13, accessed May 29, 2015.

10. W. H. Mare, "Gaza," in *The Zondervan Pictorial Encyclopedia of the Bible*, vol. 2,
D – G, ed. Merrill C. Tenney (Grand Rapids: Zondervan, 1976), 662 – 65.

Ezekiel

1.   "Food and Eating Habits," in *Illustrated Manners and Customs of the Bible*,
ed. J. I. Packer and Merrill C. Tenney (Nashville: Thomas Nelson, 1980), 469.

2.   Charles H. Dyer, "Ezekiel," in *The Bible Knowledge Commentary:
Old Testament*, ed. John F. Walvoord and Roy B. Zuck (Wheaton, Ill.: Victor
Books, 1986), 1236.

3.   NET Bible, "Diblah," http://classic.net.bible.org/dictionary.php?word=Diblah,
accessed Nov. 9, 2015.

4.   Gary G. Cohen, "Maskit," in *The Theological Wordbook of the Old Testament*,
vol. 2, ed. R. Laird Harris (Chicago: Moody Press, 1980), 876.

5.   Paul W. Gaebelein, "Tammuz," in *The International Standard Bible
Encyclopedia*, vol. 4, *Q – Z*, ed. Geoffrey Bromiley (Grand Rapids: Eerdmans,
1988), 725 – 26.

6.   R. Laird Harris, "Cherub," in *Theological Wordbook of the Old Testament*, vol. 1,
ed. R. Laird Harris (Chicago: Moody Press, 1980), 454.

7.   Dwight E. Acomb, "Cherub/Cherubim," in *The Zondervan Pictorial
Encyclopedia of the Bible*, vol. 1, *A – C*, ed. Merrill C. Tenney (Grand Rapids:
Zondervan, 1976), 788 – 90.

8.   David E. Aune, "Magic," in *The International Standard Bible Encyclopedia*,
vol. 3, *K – P*, ed. Geoffrey Bromiley (Grand Rapids: Eerdmans, 1979), 215.

9.   Roger L. Omanson, "Phylactery," in *The International Standard Bible
Encyclopedia*, vol. 3, *K – P*, 864.

10. NET Bible, "Notes on Ezekiel," https://lumina.bible.org/bible/Ezekiel+18, Ezekiel 18:2, textual note 1, accessed Nov. 30, 2015.

11. Thomas L. Constable, "Notes on Ezekiel," 2015 ed., Sonic Light, http://soniclight.com/constable/notes/pdf/ezekiel.pdf, notes 18:1–2, 3, accessed Nov. 9, 2015.

12. Dyer, "Ezekiel," in *The Bible Knowledge Commentary: Old Testament*, 1265.

13. Dyer, "Ezekiel," in *The Bible Knowledge Commentary: Old Testament*, 1304.

14. Constable, "Notes on Ezekiel," note 40:38–41.

Daniel

1. A. W. Morton, "Education in Biblical Times," in *The Zondervan Pictorial Encyclopedia of the Bible*, vol. 2, *D–G*, ed. Merrill C. Tenney (Grand Rapids: Zondervan, 1976), 206–15.

2. W. C. Kaiser, Jr., "Name," in *The Zondervan Pictorial Encyclopedia of the Bible*, vol. 4, *M–P*, ed. Merrill C. Tenney (Grand Rapids: Zondervan, 1976), 362–63.

3. Thomas L. Constable, "Notes on Daniel," 2015 ed., Sonic Light, http://soniclight.com/constable/notes/htm/OT/Daniel/Daniel.htm, note 1.6–7, accessed June 15, 2015.

4. Merrill F. Unger, "Dream," in *The New Unger's Bible Dictionary*, ed. R. K. Harrison (Chicago: Moody Press, 1988), 317–18.

5. Unger, "Aramaic," in *The New Unger's Bible Dictionary*, 92.

6. Unger, "Furnace," in *The New Unger's Bible Dictionary*, 447.

7. W. White Jr., "Den of Lions," in *The Zondervan Pictorial Encyclopedia of the Bible*, vol. 2, *D–G*, 101.

8. Unger, "Winds," in *The New Unger's Bible Dictionary*, 1366.

9. Unger, "Throne," in *The New Unger's Bible Dictionary*, 1278–79.

10. For a more detailed explanation of these two dynasties, see John F. Walvoord and Roy B. Zuck, eds., *The Bible Knowledge Commentary: Old Testament* (Wheaton, Ill.: Victor Books, 1986), 1367–72.

Hosea

1. Thomas L. Constable, "Notes on Hosea," 2015 ed., Sonic Light, http://soniclight.com/constable/notes/htm/OT/Hosea/Hosea.htm, note 1:2, accessed Nov. 10, 2015.

2.   NET Bible, "Notes on Song of Solomon," https://lumina.bible.org/bible/
Song+of+Songs+2, Song of Solomon 2:5, syntax note 20, accessed Nov. 10, 2015.

Joel

1.   "Locust," in *National Geographic*, http://animals.nationalgeographic.com/
animals/bugs/locust/, accessed Aug. 20, 2015.

2.   Carol Kaesuk Yoon, "Looking Back at the Days of the Locust," in *New York
Times*, http://www.nytimes.com/2002/04/23/science/looking-back-at-the-days-of
-the-locust.html?pagewanted=1&pagewanted=all, accessed Aug. 20, 2015.

3.   J. I. Packer and Merrill C. Tenney, eds., "The Animals and Plants of
Palestine," in *Illustrated Manners and Customs of the Bible* (Nashville: Thomas
Nelson, 1980), 242–44.

4.   Ronald B. Allen, "Atzar," in *The Theological Wordbook of the Old Testament*,
vol. 2, ed. Robert Laird Harris, Gleason Archer, and Bruce K. Waltke (Chicago:
Moody Press, 1980), 691.

5.   Robert B. Chisolm, Jr., "Joel," in *The Bible Knowledge Commentary: Old
Testament*, ed. John F. Walvoord and Roy B. Zuck (Wheaton, Ill.: Victor Books,
1986), 1422.

Amos

1.   Donald R. Sunukjian, "Amos," in *The Bible Knowledge Commentary: Old
Testament*, ed. John F. Walvoord and Roy B. Zuck (Wheaton, Ill.: Victor Books,
1986), 1428.

2.   "Places of the Bible," in *Illustrated Manners and Customs of the Bible*,
ed. J. I. Packer and Merrill C. Tenney (Nashville: Thomas Nelson, 1980), 687.

3.   Sunukjian, "Amos," in *The Bible Knowledge Commentary: Old Testament*, 1439.

4.   Thomas L. Constable, "Notes on Amos," 2015 ed., Sonic Light,
http://soniclight.com/constable/notes/htm/OT/Amos/Amos.htm, note 3:3,
accessed Aug. 10, 2015.

5.   Sunukjian, "Amos," in *The Bible Knowledge Commentary: Old Testament*, 1442.

Jonah

1.   C. J. Davey and K. L. McKay, "Ships and Boats," in *New Bible Dictionary*,
2nd ed., ed. J. D. Douglas, and others (Wheaton, Ill.: Tyndale House, 1982),
1106, 1107.

2. J. T. Clemons, "Suicide," in *The International Standard Bible Encyclopedia*, vol. 4, Q–Z, ed. Geoffrey W. Bromiley (Grand Rapids: Eerdmans, 1988), 652.

3. "The Animals and Insects of Palestine," in *Illustrated Manners and Customs of the Bible*, ed. J. I. Packer and Merrill C. Tenney (Nashville: Thomas Nelson, 1980), 237.

4. Diadorus Siculus, *The Library of History of Diodorus Siculus*, http://penelope .uchicago.edu/Thayer/E/Roman/Texts/Diodorus_Siculus/2A*.html#ref4, accessed July 28, 2015.

5. Thomas L. Constable, "Notes on Jonah," 2015 ed., Sonic Light, http://soniclight.com/constable/notes/htm/OT/Jonah/Jonah.htm, note 3:3, accessed May 18, 2015.

Micah

1. Bruce Waltke, "Micah," in *The Minor Prophets: An Exegetical and Expository Commentary*, vol. 2, ed. Thomas Edward McComiskey (Grand Rapids: Baker Books, 1999), 625.

2. John A. Martin, "Micah," in *The Bible Knowledge Commentary: Old Testament*, ed. John F. Walvoord and Roy B. Zuck (Wheaton, Ill.: Victor Books, 1986), 1479.

3. Robert L. Alden, "Oy," in *Theological Wordbook of the Old Testament*, vol. 1, ed. R. Laird Harris (Chicago: Moody Press, 1980), 19.

4. Carl Philip Weber, "Hoy," in *Theological Wordbook of the Old Testament*, vol. 1, 212.

5. Francis Brown, S. R. Driver, and Charles A. Briggs, *The Brown-Driver-Briggs Hebrew and English Lexicon* (Peabody, Mass.: Hendrickson, 2006), 222–23.

6. Waltke, "Micah," in *The Minor Prophets*, vol. 2, 635.

7. K. G. Jung, "Asherah," in *The International Standard Bible Encyclopedia*, vol. 1, A–D, ed. Geoffrey Bromiley (Grand Rapids: Eerdmans, 1979), 317–18.

8. Waltke, "Micah," in *The Minor Prophets*, vol. 2, 745.

Zephaniah

1. "The Animals and Insects of Palestine," in *Illustrated Manners and Customs of the Bible*, ed. J. I. Packer and Merrill C. Tenney (Nashville: Thomas Nelson, 1980), 238.

2.   Thomas L. Constable, "Notes on Zephaniah," 2015 ed., Sonic Light, http://soniclight.com/constable/notes/pdf/zephaniah.pdf, note 1:10, accessed Nov. 13, 2015.

3.   NET Bible, "Notes on Zephaniah," https://lumina.bible.org/bible/Zephaniah+1, Zephaniah 1, syntax note 31, accessed Nov. 13, 2015.

4.   Merrill F. Unger, "Music," in *The New Unger's Bible Dictionary*, ed. R. K. Harrison (Chicago: Moody Press, 1988), 893–94.

Zechariah

1.   R. E. Hayden, "Persia," in *The International Standard Bible Encyclopedia*, vol. 3, *K–P*, gen. ed. Geoffrey W. Bromiley (Grand Rapids: Eerdmans, 1988), 778.

2.   Hayden, "Persia," in *The International Standard Bible Encyclopedia*, vol. 3, *K–P*, 778.

3.   NET Bible, "Notes on Deuteronomy," https://lumina.bible.org/bible/Deuteronomy+32, Deuteronomy 32:10, textual note 22, accessed Nov. 24, 2015.

4.   NET Bible, "Notes on Zechariah," https://lumina.bible.org/bible/Zechariah+2, Zechariah 2:8, textual note 10, accessed Nov. 24, 2015.

5.   Thomas L. Constable, "Notes on Zechariah," 2015 ed., Sonic Light, http://soniclight.com/constable/notes/pdf/zechariah.pdf, note 2:8–9, accessed Nov. 24, 2015.

6.   Elmer B. Smick, "Mahalasa," in *The Theological Wordbook of the Old Testament*, vol. 1, ed. Robert Laird Harris, Gleason Archer, and Bruce K. Waltke (Chicago: Moody Press, 1980), 292.

7.   F. Duane Lindsey, "Zechariah," in *The Bible Knowledge Commentary: Old Testament*, ed. John F. Walvoord and Roy B. Zuck (Wheaton, Ill.: Victor Books, 1986), 1561.

8.   NET Bible, "Notes on Zechariah," https://lumina.bible.org/bible/Zechariah+7, Zechariah 7:3–5, textual note 4, accessed Nov. 24, 2015.

9.   NET Bible, "Notes on Zechariah," https://lumina.bible.org/bible/Zechariah+7, Zechariah 7:3–5, textual note 5, accessed Nov. 24, 2015.

10. NET Bible, "Notes on Zechariah," https://lumina.bible.org/bible/Zechariah+8, Zechariah 8:19, textual note 5, accessed Nov. 24, 2015.

11. Constable, "Notes on Zechariah," note 9:1–2.

12. William Sanford LaSor, "Hadrach," in *The International Standard Bible Encyclopedia*, vol. 2, *E–J*, ed. Geoffrey W. Bromiley (Grand Rapids: Eerdmans, 1988), 592.

13. Ronald F. Youngblood, "Teraphim," in *The Theological Wordbook of the Old Testament*, vol. 2, ed. Robert Laird Harris, Gleason Archer, and Bruce K. Waltke (Chicago: Moody Press, 1980), 980–81.

14. NET Bible, "Notes on Zechariah," https://lumina.bible.org/bible/Zechariah+12, Zechariah 12:11, textual note 17, accessed Nov. 28, 2015.

15. Lindsey, "Zechariah," in *The Bible Knowledge Commentary: Old Testament*, 1567.

16. NET Bible, "Notes on Zechariah," textual note 17.

17. Lindsey, "Zechariah," in *The Bible Knowledge Commentary: Old Testament*, 1568.

18. Adapted from Wayne Stiles, "Mount of Olives—The Place of God's Coming, Going, and Coming," http://www.waynestiles.com/mount-of-olives-the-place-of-gods-coming-going-and-coming/, accessed Nov. 30, 2015.

Malachi

1. Thomas L. Constable, "Notes on Malachi," 2015 ed., Sonic Light, http://soniclight.org/constable/notes/pdf/malachi.pdf, note 1.7, accessed Nov. 11, 2015.

2. Richard D. Patterson, "The Widow, Orphan, and the Poor in the Old Testament and the Extra-Biblical Literature," *Bibliotheca Sacra* (July 1973) (Dallas: Dallas Theological Seminary, 1973), 223–34.

3. Constable, "Notes on Malachi," note 3.16.

4. Craig A. Blaising, "Malachi," in *The Bible Knowledge Commentary: Old Testament*, ed. John F. Walvoord and Roy B. Zuck (Wheaton, Ill.: Victor Books, 1986), 1586.

RESOURCES FOR PROBING FURTHER

The principles and power of the Word of God are timeless, yet at times the setting, references, and practices within the Bible were set in particular times and places. We are fortunate to have access to scholarship that helps contextualize and better understand the Bible. Keep in mind that we cannot always endorse everything a writer or ministry says, so we encourage you to approach these and all other non-biblical resources with wisdom and discernment.

Arnold, Clinton E., and others, eds. *Zondervan Illustrated Bible Backgrounds Commentary*, 4 vols. Grand Rapids: Zondervan, 2002.

Bromiley, Geoffrey, W., and others, eds. *The International Standard Bible Encyclopedia*, 4 vols. Grand Rapids: Eerdmans, 1995.

Grudem, Wayne, C. John Collins, and Thomas R. Schreiner, eds. *Understanding Scripture: An Overview of the Bible's Origin, Reliability, and Meaning*. Wheaton, Ill.: Crossway, 2012.

Insight for Living. *Insight's Bible Handbook: Practical Helps for Bible Study*. Plano, Tex.: IFL Publishing House, 2010.

Kaiser, Walter C., Jr. *The Old Testament Documents: Are They Reliable and Relevant?* Downers Grove, Ill.: IVP Academic, 2001.

Marshall, I. Howard, and others, eds. *New Bible Dictionary*, 3d ed. Downers Grove, Ill.: InterVarsity, 1996.

Packer, J. I., and M. C. Tenney, eds. *Illustrated Manners and Customs of the Bible*. Nashville: Thomas Nelson, 1980.

Walvoord, John F., and Roy B. Zuck, eds. *The Bible Knowledge Commentary: An Exposition of the Scriptures by Dallas Seminary Faculty, Old Testament Edition*. Wheaton, Ill.: Victor Books, 1986.

ORDERING INFORMATION

If you would like to order additional copies of *Insight's Handbook of Old Testament Backgrounds: Key Customs from Each Book, Job—Malachi* or other Insight for Living Ministries' resources, please contact the office that serves you.

United States

Insight for Living Ministries
Post Office Box 5000
Frisco, Texas 75034-0055
USA
1-800-772-8888
(Monday through Friday, 7:00 a.m.–7:00 p.m. central time)
www.insight.org
www.insightworld.org

Canada

Insight for Living Canada
PO Box 8 Stn A
Abbotsford BC V2T 6Z4
CANADA
1-800-663-7639
www.insightforliving.ca

Australia, New Zealand, and South Pacific

Insight for Living Australia
Post Office Box 443
Boronia, VIC 3155
AUSTRALIA
+61 3 9762 6613
www.ifl.org.au

United Kingdom and Europe

Insight for Living United Kingdom
PO Box 553
Dorking
RH4 9EU
UNITED KINGDOM
0800 787 9364
+44 1306 640156
www.insightforliving.org.uk

Other International Locations

International constituents may contact the U.S. office through our Web site (www.insightworld.org), mail queries, or by calling +1-972-473-5136.

SCRIPTURE INDEX

Deuteronomy

Joshua

Judges

2 Kings

1 Chronicles

2 Chronicles

Ezra

Jeremiah

Lamentations

Ezekiel

Obadiah

Jonah

Micah

Nahum

Habakkuk

Zephaniah

Haggai

Zechariah

SUBJECT INDEX